A DIVINE REVELATION of PRAYER

Other Titles by Mary K. Baxter

A Divine Revelation of Angels
A Divine Revelation of Deliverance
A Divine Revelation of Heaven
A Divine Revelation of Hell
A Divine Revelation of Spiritual Warfare
A Divine Revelation of the Spirit Realm
The Power of the Blood
(all titles also available in Spanish)

Other Titles by George G. Bloomer

Authority Abusers
Crazy House, Sane House
(with Jeannie Bloomer)
Empowered from Above
Looking for Love
Love, Dating, and Marriage: Tough Questions, Honest Answers
More of Him
Spiritual Warfare
Witchcraft in the Pews

Mary K. Baxter
with George Bloomer

A Divine Revelation of Prayer

A DIVINE REVELATION OF PRAYER

Evangelist Mary K. Baxter
Divine Revelation, Inc
P.O. Box 121524
West Melbourne, FL 32912-1524
www.adivinerevelation.org

George G. Bloomer
Bethel Family Worship Center
515 Dowd Street
Durham, NC 27701
www.bethelfamily.org

ISBN-13: 978-1-60374-050-0 • ISBN-10: 1-60374-050-3
Printed in the United States of America

Whitaker House
1030 Hunt Valley Circle
New Kensington, PA 15068
www.whitakerhouse.com

Library of Congress Cataloging-in-Publication Data

Baxter, Mary K.
A divine revelation of prayer / by Mary K. Baxter with George G. Bloomer.
p. cm.
Summary: "Describes spiritual visions relating to answered prayer and deliverance, how to pray, and what to do if your prayers do not seem to be answered"—Provided by publisher.
ISBN 978-1-60374-050-0 (trade pbk. : alk. paper) 1. Prayer—Christianity. 2. Private revelations. I. Bloomer, George G., 1963- II. Title.
BV210.3.B39 2008
248.3'2—dc22 2008021439

1 2 3 4 5 6 7 8 9 10 ш 14 13 12 11 10 09 08

Contents

PREFACE

Do you realize how important you are to God? Your existence is so vital that it says in the Scriptures:

> *Then God said, "Let Us make man in Our image, according to Our likeness; let them have dominion over the fish of the sea, over the birds of the air, and over the cattle, over all the earth and over every creeping thing that creeps on the earth." So God created man in His own image; in the image of God He created him; male and female He created them.* (Genesis 1:26–27)

> *You have made* [man] *a little lower than the angels, and You have crowned him with glory and honor. You have made him to have dominion over the works of Your hands.* (Psalm 8:5–6)

Even though God honored human beings and entrusted them with dominion over the things that He created, humanity's ability to have dominion was disrupted when the first man and woman disobeyed His command and rejected His ways. We therefore need a restored relationship with God through Christ in order to exercise true authority in the earth. In addition, our effectiveness and walk of faith are only as strong as our prayer lives and commitment to God.

Prayer Is Essential for Our Lives

When you begin talking to God and fellowshipping with Him, He responds and gives you His wisdom and knowledge. He shows you who you really are in Christ, and He gives you the power and boldness that you need to intercede for a change not only in your own life, but also in the lives of those around you. Why? Because His powerful anointing affects all who come into its presence.

Today, many people are looking for spiritual enlightenment and a renewed way of thinking about life in general. Most do not know that they are really seeking a restored relationship with God, the heavenly Father, through the Lord Jesus Christ. The harvest of spiritual seekers is great, but many of God's laborers have grown tired and fallen by the wayside. More than ever, prayer is essential for our lives and the lives of others. Without prayer and God's Word, which connect us to the heart and mind of God, we are left to our own imaginations and self-destructive habits.

God longs for us to come to Him for divine guidance. He seizes opportunities to answer us because in doing so, He is glorified. The Lord does not want us to be left to our own devices. Instead, He admonishes us to seek Him in all things. *"In all your ways acknowledge Him, and He shall direct your paths"* (Proverbs 3:6). We need to recognize God's sovereignty and omnipotent ability to give us the answers that we seek.

Many times, we are so busy trying to figure out if God is going to answer our prayers that we unknowingly become hindrances to them by getting in the way and trying to "help" God bless us. He longs to be the Supplier of all our needs. So God does not need our help in blessing us, but He does need us to become obedient vessels, fit for the Master's use, ready and willing to carry out His commands for the work of His kingdom.

God Holds the Key

Prayer has the ability to show us both our weaknesses and God's strength. As we are open and honest before God, prayer reveals the real "us." Nothing is hidden—not even the things we wish He couldn't see. He sees and knows everything about us, yet prayer will reveal our weaknesses to us so that we will look to Him for His strength.

Despite our weaknesses and failures, God loves us. When we rely on Him, trusting in the work of Christ to save and empower us, He enables us to be what He has created us to be. Sometimes, we rely on our own words rather than God's power. It is time to let go of religious jargon and embrace the Spirit and omnipotence of God. As we rest in the knowledge that He is our Supplier and lean on His strength and provision, we begin to experience His miraculous works.

A Divine Revelation of Prayer will give you the reassurance of knowing that God has your best interests at heart, even when it seems as if your prayers are not being answered. Continue to "acknowledge Him" and believe in Him as the all-powerful Father. He holds the key that unlocks the door to provision for your every need. Not only does God have the means to meet your need, but also, amazingly enough, if you have sought His will in prayer, with faith, your prayers have already been accomplished in the spiritual realm. (See Mark 11:24.) You are simply waiting for the manifestation of what you have prayed for to appear in the physical realm.

There is no reason to be intimidated by circumstances when you have been given access to the wisdom and power of your God. With a regular prayer life, you can have peace instead of panic in the midst of turmoil. A 2003 Gallup poll revealed that only 35 percent of American Christians have "inner contentment even when things go wrong."[1] How can we get this percentage to increase? By obeying this instruction from the Word of God and encouraging others to do the same: always pray and don't lose heart. (See Luke 18:1.)

[1] George H. Gallup Jr., "How Are American Christians Living Their Faith?" http://www.gallup.com/poll/9088/How-American-Christians-Living-Their-Faith.aspx (accessed March 7, 2008).

Introduction

by Mary K. Baxter

Some of the most intimate times that I have had with God have occurred during periods of great travail in prayer. It is during these times that God reveals Himself to me in visions, and I am so grateful for having the opportunity to share these mighty visions throughout the world to set the captives free. I am always grateful to God when He reveals to me His secrets through prayer. I rejoice in knowing that He trusts me to engage in spiritual warfare against the kingdom of darkness and to intercede for His mighty acts to be fulfilled. I have learned that everything God reveals to us is important and has a purpose—including the things that are written in His Scriptures, which we often take for granted.

The Nature and Power of Prayer

Prayer Helps Build a Relationship with God

Many of the things that God showed me during my visions did not actually come to pass in the natural until years later. That is why I always like to stress the nature and power of prayer. Unless we talk to God and learn to recognize His voice, we become impatient when things in life do not go as we had planned. As we build a relationship with God, however, we learn to live in a place of contentment where, regardless of what is going on around us, we can see beyond the natural sphere and into the spiritual realm. God always has a bigger picture and a better plan than we can fathom.

Prayer Has No Boundaries

I have also learned that prayer has no boundaries. I have often called upon intercessors to agree with me in prayer, and whether they were sitting beside me or miles away on the phone, the result remained the same: God heard and answered. Once, while praying with an intercessor whom I'd recently met, I realized that she was the person I'd had a vision about years prior to our meeting! This and other miraculous occurrences are included in the chapters that follow, along with divine revelation of what is actually taking place in the spiritual realm while we pray, so that you can build your faith and have your own amazing experiences with God through prayer. For instance, we don't realize how pleased God is when we submit ourselves as living sacrifices to Him, and how He receives us upon His altar in heaven.

Prayer Needs to Be Combined with a Pure Heart

God is holy, and it is vital to approach the Lord in prayer with a pure heart. This does not mean that you will never wrestle with issues, because God gave us the gift of prayer as a means to communicate with Him and to receive His help and healing in the midst of our many personal struggles. Going to God with a pure heart means that your intentions are without guile or bitterness. For instance, you wouldn't want to go to the most holy God just because you were angry at your brother or sister and ask the Lord to bring misfortune in that person's life. This displeases God, and it is not what God designed prayer to accomplish.

Prayer Needs to Be Combined with God's Word

The Word of God is truth. It is to be respected, and it is to be the basis of our prayers. It is the spiritual Manual that He has given us as a weapon against the kingdom of darkness. Again, God has a purpose for everything He has written in His Word. He wants us to include His Word in our prayers, in order to show Him we are trusting in His promises and are expecting Him to fulfill them. We also must know His Word so that we can counteract the accusations the devil brings against us. (See Romans 8:1; Revelation 12:10–11.) Finally, the Word helps us to become familiar with God's ways so we will not become vulnerable to the deception and false teachings of others, who can be wolves in sheep's clothing. (See Matthew 7:15.)

Prayer Reveals God's Will

Not only that, but as we learn to talk with God, we also find out what we are meant to be and do in our lives. Perhaps you have wondered, *God, what is my calling; what is my purpose? Why have You placed me on this earth? What is the larger picture for my existence?* The answers to these and many other questions can be found by diligently seeking the Lord in prayer. God has a purpose for our existence. Though we may not always understand Him, He is always ready to lead us, even in our reluctance to follow. I want you to know that God loves you and continually has your best interests at heart. When you know your purpose and become diligent in fulfilling it, you allow nothing or no one to get in the way of accomplishing what God has shown you by His Spirit.

Diligence is a must because, again, God does not always manifest answers to prayer right away. He allows us to go through certain experiences in life so that when He does present us with an answer, we are capable of handling what He says and does. God knows that we are not yet ready to handle some of the things that we *think* we can handle. Therefore, He shields us, just as a parent shields a child who is learning to take her first steps into a new stage of life. Prayer equips you with the ability to receive God's divine guidance and not to become weary in doing good. (See 2 Thessalonians 3:13.)

My prayer for you as you read this book is that you will be filled with the anointing of God, that you will gain a greater revelation of God's omnipotence, and that you will receive an outpouring of His Spirit as never before. I praise God that *A Divine Revelation of Prayer* will go all over the world and set people free. I thank the Lord that I can share with you the nuggets He has given to me. God bless you. I love you very much.

Dear Heavenly Father,

May Your power touch the person who is reading this book. May he or she feel Your anointing with every page. I pray that whatever strongholds have been binding this individual and his or her family will be loosed in the name of Jesus. May this book be a weapon to transform lives for Your glory and honor. May Your peace, which passes all human understanding, fill Your people, and may we find Your sanctity in our hearts. Father, I come against the kingdom of darkness, against the principalities and powers that have been blinding Your people from seeing You in all Your glory. May we be continually enlightened, and may our growth in You increase as never before!

In Jesus' name, amen.

—Mary K. Baxter

Introduction

by George G. Bloomer

As a pastor, I am often confronted with the question, "Bishop Bloomer, why hasn't God answered my prayers?" While there may be a number of reasons for a seeming delay in answered prayer, these truths are very clear: (1) God wants us to pray, (2) He desires to reveal Himself to us, and (3) He wants to answer our prayers:

> *This is what the Lord says, he who made the earth, the Lord who formed it and established it—the Lord is his name: "Call to me and I will answer you and tell you great and unsearchable things you do not know."* (Jeremiah 33:2–3 NIV)

> *Whatever things you ask when you pray, believe that you receive them, and you will have them.* (Mark 11:24)

This book explores reasons why your prayers don't seem to be answered, so you can move past doubt and confusion and strengthen your faith in God and His purposes. It also reveals what occurs in the heavenly realm when you pray, and how God wants to use your prayers to effect His will in the world.

Prayer Brings Spiritual Help and Cultural Transformation

We hear so much about "the power of prayer" that many Christians have become complacent about it. Yet this phrase is not a cliché. The power of prayer is real. God is so intent on answering our prayers that He has gifted us with a direct path to His heart. For Jesus promised, *"If you ask anything in My name, I will do it"* (John 14:14).

I often pray and intercede for individuals who seem shocked when the answers to their prayers finally arrive. We have become so accustomed to saying words that we sometimes forget that we are communicating with an all-knowing and all-powerful God. When you pray, your prayers are heard in heaven, and God sends His angels to do His bidding on your behalf. You must realize that prayer is not a ritual. It is not just talking to yourself. It is a powerful vehicle for personal spiritual help as well as cultural transformation.

Prayer Strengthens Us for Spiritual Warfare

When you pray and commit your concerns to God, you become an awesome threat to the devil's kingdom because he knows that you will not go down without a fight. The devil realizes that he is no longer fighting a mere man or woman, but instead One within you who is infinitely greater than he. (See 1 John 4:4.) He knows his strategy must become much more cunning and deceptive to accomplish his purposes. He wants to cause you to walk away from God long enough to inflict his demonic damage. He attempts to put more on you than you think you can bear, in hopes that you will begin to question your God, give up, and even renounce your faith. Don't fall for it! *"Be steadfast, immovable, always abounding in the work of the Lord, knowing that your labor is not in vain in the Lord"* (1 Corinthians 15:58). God recognizes perseverance and is a Rewarder of those who continue to diligently seek Him in prayer. (See Hebrews 11:6.)

The spiritual battle we are engaged in is much like a boxing match. Once a boxer sees his opponent's weakness, he uses it to his advantage. He begins pounding at the spot where he has already inflicted the most damage because he knows that it will be only a matter of time before his opponent buckles to his knees.

The devil has the same strategy. Whether it's your health, your family, your career, your finances, or another aspect of your life, he will study the area where the most damage seems to have been inflicted and continue pounding it, waiting patiently for you to surrender to him. Your job is to tell the devil that the only person to whom you will surrender is God, and for Him only will you fall to your knees!

My prayer for you is that you will have faith, perseverance, and power:

> Father God,
>
> I come against every demonic distraction that will attempt to hinder Your revelation from going forth to the reader of this book. I pray that even now his or her life will begin to change. May Your people gain a greater knowledge of Your power, and may their faith be built up. I pray that You will open their spirits to You, and that they will begin to see the manifestation of Your Word in action. Lord, cover them and give them a deeper revelation of the power of prayer. Anoint them with power, not only for themselves, but also for others, so that they may lay hands on the sick and see them recover, rebuke the devil and bring deliverance

to the oppressed, and proclaim the gospel for the salvation of many. May the anointing of Your Holy Spirit be "contagious" to all who come in contact with Your people from this day forth.

In Jesus' name, amen.

—George G. Bloomer

Chapter 1

Is God Really Listening?

Do you ever feel as if God isn't listening? Do your prayers seem to have gone unanswered? Many Christians who are seeking a deeper relationship with God, as well as more effective service for Him, secretly struggle with an inner battle between faith in God and uncertainty that He will answer their prayers. We wrestle with our sinful nature, the attacks of Satan, and life's trials. If we continually expect to see physical results as soon as we rise from our knees in prayer, the tendency to doubt God can become a recurring habit. Yet we can be encouraged by knowing that even though we do not visibly see God at work, He is actively answering our requests in the spiritual realm.

Time and distance are no match for Almighty God. Some of the prayers you prayed years ago are just beginning to manifest.

> *Beloved, do not forget this one thing, that with the Lord one day is as a thousand years, and a thousand years as one day. The Lord is not slack concerning His promise.* (2 Peter 3:8–9)

A Startling Discovery

There is a world beyond what we can see physically. And there are spiritual activities going on in the earthly realm that are totally invisible to those who live in the finite world of humanity. Some years ago, I was praising the Lord while going about the day's business when suddenly the Lord spoke to me and said, "Start praying." I started praying and praying in the Spirit. I asked God, "Lord, what is this?" and again I continued interceding. A vision appeared before me of an airplane circling over the ocean. I watched and said, "Oh, my God! Something is wrong with the plane." I didn't understand all of this. I just prayed and prayed for almost four hours, and then the vision lifted. I continued going about my daily chores, and then my children came home from school. After that incident, every once in a while, I would think of that prayer, so I wrote it down.

Years went by, and we eventually moved to another state. There I met a dear friend of mine, and we were talking about experiences with God and having a good time in the Lord. I shared with her, "Once I had a vision, but I never got an answer to it. I did not hear anything about it on television or anything, but in the vision I saw a plane circling over the ocean, and I knew the plane was in danger." All of a sudden my friend looked startled. "What did you say? What did you say?" she kept asking. So I told her again and she said, "I was on that plane."

Even when we don't visibly see God at work, He is answering our requests in the spiritual realm.

"What do you mean?" I asked.

"My husband was in the military. We were stationed overseas, and I had to fly on this plane with one of the children coming back into America. In flight, we were told by the pilot that there was a problem with the plane and we had to circle over the ocean because we couldn't land until they let us. This went on until they finally let us land and we got off the plane, but we never knew the amount of danger we were in. They told us later that there had actually been a bomb on that plane. When they finally found it in a suitcase, they took it out over the ocean and dropped the suitcase in the water and the bomb went off. I was so afraid when I was on that plane, and I was praying to God to spare my life."

I responded, "This happened twenty years ago, and even though I was in Michigan and you were flying back from in Saudi Arabia, God connected us to pray because you called on the Lord to help you. He saw an intercessor who prayed, and because of that, not only was your life spared, but the lives of everyone on the whole airplane."

"Yes," she answered, "an entire airplane filled with people."

All I could say was, "What a God we serve!" Only God could hear—and answer—the prayers of His servant. What the devil meant for evil, God turned around for His glory.

What the devil meant for evil, God turned around for His glory.

This is the same God you serve. Think of Him as the Great Physician. He has already diagnosed your ailment and prescribed the cure for whatever your needs and concerns are. All He asks in return is that you trust Him and follow His instructions. In the physical world, when your medical doctor prescribes medicine for an ailment, you do not always know what ingredients you're taking.

However, you trust in the expertise of the physician and take your daily dose as instructed. You believe that you will be healed, or at least relieved, of your malady. You may not immediately feel the results, but you know that as you continue taking the medication according to the instructions, your body will eventually begin to respond and heal.

Exercising this same patience and diligence regarding the things of God, however, can sometimes seem much more challenging. Why is it so easy to trust natural physicians yet seemingly so hard to trust the Healer of the world—our Lord and Savior—so that we continually doubt Him?

Reasons Prayers Don't Seem to Be Answered

The Season Has Not Yet Come

One reason our prayers may not seem to be answered is that the season has not yet come for God to reveal the full manifestation of the answer. Some prayers are answered more swiftly than others. God does not make mistakes in His answers or His timing: *"To everything there is a season, a time for every purpose under heaven"* (Ecclesiastes 3:1).

There is a time and a season for everything—God's appointed time. A seeming delay in an answer to prayer does not indicate that He hasn't heard us, nor does it mean that He has not answered. We can rest assured that He has heard every word. Yet He is not pressured to "hurry up" and show us a sign in order to prove His presence and power to act on our behalf. We just have to trust Him and know that when we pray according to His will, what He has already completed in the invisible realm will be manifested upon the earth, as well.

Though the "vision" sometimes tarries, you must still wait for it because, at its appointed time, it will surely come. (See Habakkuk 2:3.) In other words, the things that God has shown you, the things that He has promised, and the things that are ordained by Him will come to pass.

Demonic Interference

Just because we do not see the physical manifestation of our prayers in action does not mean that God has not answered. A classic example of this truth is revealed in the book of Daniel. Daniel was humbly praying to God for three weeks as he sought understanding and guidance about a vision he had been given about the future of the Israelites. His answer came after those weeks, and the angel who brought him the answer explained that Daniel had been heard the first day he had begun to pray. The angel also said that he was sent in response to Daniel's prayer, but that he had been held up while fighting against strong demonic forces that were resisting him. (See Daniel 10:1–14.)

Therefore, we may not receive an immediate answer to our prayers because of demonic resistance, and we must continue to pray and perhaps engage in spiritual warfare before seeing the answer. As you pray and intercede, you will receive a breakthrough. No demon or principality from hell can stop God's purpose from being fulfilled.

What God has promised and ordained will come to pass.

I remember getting up bright and early one morning to intercede for one of my sisters, who lived in Oklahoma at the time. Again, this was years ago when my children were still young, so after getting them off to school, I went into prayer. I was holding my stomach and praying like a woman having a baby, and I just kept praying and praying for hours. The phone would ring or someone would knock on the door, but I wouldn't allow anything or anyone to distract me. I just kept pressing and travailing for her in the Lord. I made up my mind that nothing was going to hinder me from interceding until I received a breakthrough.

I went to the top of the stairs and sat down. I put my hands over my eyes, hung my head, and said, "God, my sister needs prayer so bad." All at once, I had a vision. I saw her home, and inside it I saw a big, thick, black blanket-like covering in her bedroom hovering over her and her husband. As I continued looking at it, it began to descend upon them and try to smother them. Suddenly, I saw angels come in the room with swords drawn and fire coming out of the swords. The angels began removing that dark shadow, and it disintegrated. The angels were praising the Lord, and I felt relief from the prayer. Later, she shared with me how it felt as if something had attempted to smother them to death. God had used me to pray against this demonic attack.

Ill-conceived Prayer

Some prayers are not answered at all in the sense that we do not receive what we specifically ask for. However, this does not mean that God has not heard us and that the Spirit is not interceding on our behalf. (See Romans 8:26.) When you pray with the mind-set that God's will is going to be fulfilled in your life, you thank Him for caring about you so much that He does not answer requests that would be bad for you in the long run. God generously answers the prayers that promote our good, not our harm.

Praying without Expecting

Another reason prayer may not show results is that when you continue to pray without expectation of an answer, you eventually develop doubt, and a lack of faith blocks answers to prayer.

> *But without faith it is impossible to please Him, for he who comes to God must believe that He is, and that He is a rewarder of those who diligently seek Him.*
>
> (Hebrews 11:6)

God is concerned about our needs being met, and He rejoices when we exercise our faith in Him through prayer. In Matthew 7, the Lord reminds us that when we earnestly seek Him, He does not ignore us, but He gives us the desires of our hearts, according to His perfect will.

> *Ask, and it will be given to you; seek, and you will find; knock, and it will be opened to you. For everyone who asks receives, and he who seeks finds, and to him who knocks it will be opened. Or what man is there among you who, if his son asks for bread, will give him a stone? Or if he asks for a fish, will he give him a serpent? If you then, being evil, know how to give good gifts to your children, how much*

> *more will your Father who is in heaven give good things to those who ask Him!*
> (Matthew 7:7–11)

I have learned that when I seek the Lord, He answers me. He may answer in a still small voice. (See 1 Kings 19:11–12.) He may show me in a vision, or I might get a telephone call and receive my answer from God through one of His chosen vessels because I pray in expectation. *"Now faith is the substance of things hoped for, the evidence of things not seen"* (Hebrews 11:1). If you are not receiving anything, it may be because you've stopped asking—or stopped believing.

FAITH MUST LEAD THE WAY

The conduit between prayer and manifestation is *faith*. When it seems as if God is not listening, faith must lead the way until the manifestation of what you have been praying for becomes a visible reality. This is why the devil plays tricks with our minds to make us think that God does not care: Satan wants us to become so frustrated that we begin to doubt the Lord. The result of our doubting is that we often try to self-medicate our spiritual wounds with earthly alternatives, such as escapism or taking action on impulse, which unfortunately may yield temporary relief but long-lasting bad results.

Yet Matthew 6:8 reminds us, *"Your Father knows the things you have need of before you ask Him."* Without a doubt, God is listening. If God knows what your needs are before you even ask Him, then surely He hears both your inner thoughts and those that are outwardly vocalized through prayer. You need spiritual discernment and faith to believe that He will manifest your answer in the natural world.

Jesus did the works of God on a consistent basis, and He said something astounding in John 14:12–14:

> *Most assuredly, I say to you, he who believes in Me, the works that I do he will do also; and greater works than these he will do, because I go to My Father. And whatever you ask in My name, that I will do, that the Father may be glorified in the Son. If you ask anything in My name, I will do it.*

The role of faith is to transfer us from a human way of thinking to a spiritual mind-set, so that we no longer think or act based upon our physical limitations. Rather, we accomplish seemingly impossible feats as we are led by the Spirit of God. God can't wait to answer your prayers. Many of us have heard the above words of Jesus recited on numerous occasions, but now we must truly receive them as applicable to our lives.

What is the requirement for experiencing God's divine manifestations? Believe in Jesus Christ.

What happens to those who believe? The works that Jesus did, you will be able to accomplish, also.

Because Jesus returned to God, our heavenly Father, and gave us the gift of the indwelling and empowering Holy Spirit, we who believe will continue to carry on His mission. We will do even greater works in His name, for the glory of the Father.

Can you imagine what would happen if we really believed the Word without wavering?

Whatever you ask in Jesus' name, the Lord will fulfill according to His will. Jesus loves it when we call upon His name to answer our requests. He receives it as worship, and as if we're saying, "Lord, You are sovereign, and only You can fulfill my need. I believe in You and have the faith that You are answering my prayers as only You can." Jesus repeated His desire that we use the authority of His name in prayer: *"If you ask anything in My name, I will do it"* (John 14:14).

Can you imagine what would happen to us if we really believed the Word of God without wavering? Miracles would increase in our churches; more of us would lay hands on the sick and see them recover; people would begin to take Christians seriously; and even those who hate us would not be able to deny the anointing that would reign in our lives.

This is the type of faith that David had, even before he became king of Israel. He didn't flee from challenges. David often got into trouble with his elders for coming against problems that were much bigger than he but much smaller than the God whom he served. Despite the constant criticism, David did not waver in faith when faced with adversity.

In 1 Samuel 17, David encountered the Philistine giant, Goliath, whom even the armies of Israel feared. David was just a boy at this point. Yet when he was rebuked by his oldest brother, Eliab, David did not even acknowledge the risk associated with such a challenge. Instead, he insisted, *"What have I done now? Is there not a cause?"* (1 Samuel 17:29). In other words, David demanded to know the nature of his brother's problem with him. His way of thinking was, *There is a cause that needs to be fulfilled. I don't see anyone else volunteering to take out this Philistine, so why shouldn't I just go down there and take care of him myself?*

Despite his small stature, David had faith in God. So great was his faith that he became offended by the fact that anyone would have the audacity to come against God's servants: *"For who is this uncircumcised Philistine, that he should defy the armies of the living God?"* (1 Samuel 17:26). All too often, when we undergo spiritual battles, our anger is misdirected. Instead of becoming angry at God for the circumstances we face, we should be like David and direct that anger toward God's enemy by defeating the devil with the Word of God. David was able to have faith in God because he had spent much time with Him in worship and in meditation on God's Word. In response, the Lord had already revealed and proven to David the power that he possessed through faith in Him.

Through God, therefore, David had the power to overcome obstacles much greater than he. When King Saul brought to David's attention that he was only a lad and the Philistine had been *"a man of war from his youth"* (1 Samuel 17:33), David simply responded, *"The Lord, who delivered me from the paw of the lion and from the paw of the bear, He will deliver me from the hand of this Philistine*" (1 Samuel 17:37). No one—not even the king—could dissuade David from operating by the power of God.

When you are possessed with power from on high, and you know it, there is nothing that anyone can say or do to convince you to doubt God. You don't go into prayer with wishful thinking but with great expectation. You understand that although things in the natural look impossible to defeat, God is limitless in power and might. With Him on your side, you are operating not by your own strength but by His power. "*'Not by might nor by power, but by My Spirit,' says the Lord of hosts*" (Zechariah 4:6).

Don't Lose Heart!

We all go through phases where we question whether or not God is going to show up on our behalf to defeat the giants that confront us in life. But 2 Corinthians 4 gives us the hope that we need to continue persevering:

> *Therefore we do not lose heart. Even though our outward man is perishing, yet the inward man is being renewed day by day. For our light affliction, which is but for a moment, is working for us a far more exceeding and eternal weight of*

> *glory, while we do not look at the things which are seen, but at the things which are not seen. For the things which are seen are temporary, but the things which are not seen are eternal.*
>
> (2 Corinthians 4:16–18)

This passage tells us…

- Don't lose heart.
- Regardless of what it looks like on the outside, our strength is being renewed by God within.
- The things that we face are not as big as they appear, for there is always an even greater picture of hope.
- Don't focus so much on what is going on in the natural. It's what is going on in the spiritual realm that counts.
- The things that we can see (our circumstances) are temporary, but the things that we cannot see (God working on our behalf and transforming us into the image of the Lord Jesus) are securing our eternity in glory.

It's always discouraging to see someone suddenly give up when he or she is very close to a miracle. Even when you are weak and perhaps feel as if there is a breach between you and God, the Lord will still give you what you need to persevere.

To the weak who trust Him, God gives power. To those who feel that they have utterly no might at all, He continues to increase strength. (See Isaiah 40:29.) God loves it when we talk to Him and come to Him for strength when we feel weak. God wants you to lay everything that is bothering you at His feet. *"Cast...all your care upon Him, for He cares for you"* (1 Peter 5:7). You have to take quality time with God and put Him first. And if you will put God first, He will replenish you.

God loves it when we talk to Him and ask for strength when we feel weak.

Regardless of what is taking place in your immediate surroundings, never give up on God, because He will never give up on you. *"He Himself has said, 'I will never leave you nor forsake you'"* (Hebrews 13:5). Wait on God, and you will soon possess the power to fly over every hindrance that has restrained you from rising to fulfill the call of God—the call that He has entrusted you to carry out according to His will.

> *Those who wait on the Lord shall renew their strength; they shall mount up with wings like eagles, they shall run and not be weary, they shall walk and not faint.*
> (Isaiah 40:31)

MIRACULOUS EXPERIENCES WITH GOD IN PRAYER

It's time for men, women, boys, and girls to turn back to God and pray. I have had many miraculous experiences with God in prayer, and He has proven His love for me time and again. Talking to the Father and relying upon Him for guidance helps to build a stronger relationship with Him. In addition, not only will God give you spiritual insight for your own trials, but He also will anoint you through prayer to intercede for others.

There are so many wonderful benefits in talking to our Father. I have learned that everything God reveals to us is important and has a purpose. As a servant of the Lord, my calling is in visions and revelations. Seeking God in prayer has brought forth these spiritual manifestations. I often arise early in the morning to seek His face, and I look forward to being used as His vessel to bless others and spread His gospel.

I want to encourage you and build up your faith by sharing some remarkable experiences that I have had with God through visions and the power of prayer. I get very excited when I share with others the relevance of prayer because talking to the Lord and listening to Him has transformed my life.

A type of vision that has special significance for me is one in which I have seen beams of light. These light beams were small at the bottom, but they expanded as they neared the heavens. I realized that what appeared as bright lights were actually the prayers of the people, and they were very beautiful. Angels gathered the words of these prayers onto scrolls and placed them in specific areas in heaven. Sometimes, I saw prayers that resembled thousands of sheets of paper stacked to the height of a large monument. The Lord told me they were a memorial to the intercessors of the earth who were praying with pure hearts.

God wants you to build positive experiences with Him in prayer.

Again, Satan wants to fill you with frustration and anger over the circumstances in your life, so that you not only neglect to pray for yourself, but you also refuse to pray for anyone else. He wants to keep you from seeking God for answers. I really believe that if people would turn back to God, many of the situations of this world would be forced to change. God has everything that we need, and He is prepared to bless us abundantly when we put Him first.

Letting God Take Over

You may feel as if you have been through so many heartaches and sorrows that you are at the brink of utter despair, but don't give up on God. He will cushion you as He leads you out of the thorns and thickets of the devil's snares. God will walk you through the storms. He has never failed, and He has never forsaken us. He wants you to begin building positive experiences with Him and to overcome things in your life that have been bogging you down. Perhaps you are experiencing trials, sadness, abandonment, uncertainty, confusion, or doubt. Perhaps you have certain habits that you would like to overcome, such as drug addiction, drinking, swearing, anxiety, anger, or gossiping. Our mighty God can help you overcome all of these things and more! Just talk to Him and ask Him. He has power beyond any other power on earth to deliver you if you call upon His name.

Psalm 145 expresses God's love for us:

> *The Lord is righteous in all His ways, gracious in all His works. The Lord is near to all who call upon Him, to all who call upon Him in truth. He will fulfill the desire of those who fear Him; He also will hear their cry and save them.*
>
> (Psalm 145:17–19)

The Lord is righteous and gracious *"in all His works"* (verse 17). He works in ways that are *"exceedingly abundantly above all that we ask or think"* (Ephesians 3:20). He hears and answers. When you humbly turn to God like a little child (see Matthew 18:3), you attract His blessings. He will enable you to mature in Him as you reach out to Him in prayer. That is why the devil uses whatever distractions that he possibly can to keep us from reaching out to God.

If you are away from God or have become discouraged, turning back to Him is only a prayer away. You may not know how to pray or understand everything about prayer, but that's all right. You will learn. In the meantime, pour out your heart to God and give your life completely to Him for His direction and protection.

Of course, it's vital for you first to be born again. Ask Jesus to come into your heart, forgive you of all your sins, wash you in His blood, and save your soul. Share your heart with Him. You can say, "Lord, here I am today. I've made mistakes, and I've sinned. Please forgive me through Jesus' sacrifice for me. I know You are here to help me overcome. And I know that as I draw closer to You and receive Your strength, these things will fall away and I will no longer continue to do them."

This is all God wants—earnest and honest communication. Don't stop praying to God just because you have made a mistake. As you turn to Him and He continually strengthens you, He will eventually make you an overcomer.

When you invite the Lord Jesus Christ into your life, you begin to change by the power of His presence. You begin to exude the presence of your future residence—heaven. You don't have to wait until you get to heaven to experience its tranquility; you can have the peace of heaven right here on earth. (See John 14:27.)

Open Doors to Unforgettable Experiences

Prayer is a door opener. If we would only believe the Word of the Lord without wavering, we could experience the fulfillment of many of our hopes and dreams. If we would only take a stand and talk to God, not only when we are in trouble, but also for the purpose of ongoing fellowship with Him, then our faith would be strengthened and we would not be moved easily by the devil's intimidation and deception.

The only way to see the type of positive change that many of us need in our lives is to build a stronger prayer life. I believe that as we turn back to God and begin to pray to Him as never before,

God will send us a great blessing from heaven. He will deliver our children from drugs, mend our families, and intervene for us, because He is our God, and He loves us. I pray that God will use this book to help millions overcome their hindrances and come closer to God by building a deeper relationship with Him through divine communication.

Chapter 2

The "How" Is Up to God

When we pray and struggle for a number of years without seeing the manifestation of our prayers, it can become very disheartening and a strain on our faith. Our frustration may even cause us to ignore God when He shows up with the answer. As a result, we do not receive the very thing for which we have believed and perhaps even begged God for.

Just imagine this situation: You go a car dealership to inquire about your dream car. Sitting on the lot is the car that you have imagined and longed for. Without hesitation, you rush over to the salesman to see if you qualify for financing to purchase it. Suddenly, the owner of the dealership approaches you and gives you extraordinary news: "In celebration of our fiftieth anniversary, I am going to give you this car. You owe us nothing. It's yours. You can drive it home today." Instead of rejoicing and thanking him for the gift, you argue with him, refuse to accept the car, and walk away with nothing.

As ridiculous as this scenario may seem, this is how many of us treat God without realizing it. Instead of receiving His blessings and praising Him for them, we practically get into arguments with Him about why it took Him so long to give us the answer, whether the gift is real "this time," why He gave it in the form He did, and so forth.

Dangers of Misunderstanding Prayer

In the Bible, there were people who either didn't recognize Jesus for who He was or who rejected Him. The following illustrations have implications for us today. People lose out on answers to prayer because they still fail to recognize God at work, or they reject the answers as not coming in the way they wanted.

Not Recognizing God's Answer

At the beginning of His ministry, while Jesus was getting ready to preach to a large crowd, He noticed two empty boats. Nearby, the fishermen were washing out their nets. Jesus climbed into one of the boats, which belonged to Simon Peter, and asked him to *"put out a little from the land"* (Luke 5:3).

Everything the Lord does is for a reason. Many times, the instructions given to us by God are not only for ourselves, but also are for the blessing of others. This is one reason why it is so vitally important to adhere to His commands without question. Jesus told Peter to put the boat out from the land because a blessing was about to take place—the people who had gathered would be able to hear Jesus' life-giving words from God. Then *"He sat down and taught the multitudes from the boat"* (Luke 5:3).

Jesus always has a picture in mind "above all we ask or think" (Ephesians 3:20).

It seems that whenever Jesus is on board, miracles happen. However, Peter almost allowed his frustration over his natural circumstances to cause him to miss out on the spiritual blessing God had in store for him:

> *When* [Jesus] *had stopped speaking, He said to Simon* [Peter], *"Launch out into the deep and let down your nets for a catch." But Simon answered and said to Him, "Master, we have toiled all night and caught nothing; nevertheless at Your word I will let down the net."* (Luke 5:4–5)

Peter was contradicting Jesus by saying to Him, in effect, "You want us to go fishing, but we are very experienced fishermen who have been at this all night long and still not caught anything. I don't see how Your advice is going to benefit us." Perhaps to prove his point, he decided to appease Jesus by letting down one net. Note that Jesus had told him to let down his nets—plural—but Peter let down just one net.

You might say that Peter's faith had sunk to the bottom of the sea. He and the other fishermen were very tired, and, after they had already begun washing out their nets, along comes Jesus asking them to drop the nets back down into the sea. Peter's solution was to obey only part of Jesus' command. When we start to see Jesus as an inconvenience or when we obey Him only halfheartedly, we begin to lose out on some of the greatest "catches" life has to offer.

> *And when they had done this, they caught a great number of fish, and their net was breaking. So they signaled to their partners in the other boat to come and help them. And they came and filled both the boats, so that they began to sink. When Simon Peter saw it, he fell down at Jesus' knees, saying, "Depart from me, for I am a sinful man, O Lord!"...And Jesus said to Simon, "Do not be afraid. From now on you will catch men."*
>
> (Luke 5:6–8, 10)

Jesus always has a greater picture in mind than we can see. He is *"able to do exceedingly abundantly above all that we ask or think"* (Ephesians 3:20). Peter was unprepared to receive the blessing that Jesus bestowed upon him. The physical net broke because it could not contain the abundance of God's blessing. Yet Peter was given an even greater blessing—a call upon his life that would include an abundance of souls coming into God's kingdom as Peter learned to obey Jesus and live according to God's ways.

What would you do if God instantly provided the answer for what you had secretly desired? Would you argue with Him? Would you recognize that He had given it? Would you thank and praise Him for it?

Peter apparently learned from this experience with Jesus, however. Consider the following account from Matthew:

> *When the disciples saw* [Jesus] *walking on the lake, they were terrified. "It's a ghost," they said, and cried out in fear. But Jesus immediately said to them: "Take courage! It is I. Don't be afraid." "Lord, if it's you," Peter replied, "tell me to come to you on the water." "Come," he said. Then Peter got down out of the boat, walked on the water and came toward Jesus. But when*

> *he saw the wind, he was afraid and, beginning to sink, cried out, "Lord, save me!" Immediately Jesus reached out his hand and caught him. "You of little faith," he said, "why did you doubt?" And when they climbed into the boat, the wind died down. Then those who were in the boat worshiped him, saying, "Truly you are the Son of God."* (Matthew 14:26–33 NIV)

The answer to your prayers might appear in a form you do not expect, but you should never be afraid to receive it. In this instance, the only one who had faith enough to receive was Peter, who dared to step out of the book and walk on the water with Jesus. Even then, he began to doubt when he looked at his natural circumstances rather than at Jesus. Take courage! Do not be afraid to receive your miracle from God when it appears.

Rejecting God's Answer

Some people recognize God at work in their midst, but they reject His blessing because they don't like the way in which He is working.

Bishop Bloomer tells about a beautiful Sunday morning when he had been called upon to preach at a service in which thousands of anxious onlookers were eagerly awaiting a "word" from the Lord. A soloist was called to the microphone to sing a selection before the preaching. He was not a member of the church, or even a gospel artist, but rather a famous rhythm and blues singer who was known for bellowing out hits without skipping a beat. As he approached the podium, he gave an astounding testimony of God's power to heal and deliver, and then explained to the crowd that he desperately needed a word from the Lord. As he opened his mouth to sing, the atmosphere immediately began to change. People were crying, waving their hands, calling out to God in surrender. There was no doubt about it; the anointing of God had shown up, taken over the service, and continued to hover like a delicate cloud.

We must truly believe that God knows what He is doing and has our best interests at heart.

Then, Bishop Bloomer's eye caught a group of older Christians sitting on one side. In the midst of all that was going on, they sat with their arms folded, as if in protest against God for using someone who does not ordinarily fit the mold of a person "worthy" to be used by Him. How is it that we can pray to God, "Lord, save the souls, heal the sick," but when He does it, we complain? This self-righteous indignation is one of the hidden traps that the devil uses to keep us from winning souls for God. For when we pray to the Lord, we cannot then tell Him how to answer our prayers.

Bishop Bloomer often tells his congregation, "The 'how' is not your business." In other words, the avenue through which God brings our prayers to pass is not our concern. We should simply pray and then step back and allow God to do what He does best, which is to answer our prayers according to His divine will.

Throughout the Bible, people who claimed to know God missed out on some of their greatest potential blessings because they refused to acknowledge Him and His ways. Let's look at two incidents of this from the life of Jesus.

> *Then the Jews took up stones again to stone Him. Jesus answered them, "Many good works I have shown you from My Father. For which of those works do you stone Me?" The Jews answered Him, saying, "For a good work we do not stone You, but for blasphemy, and because You, being a Man, make Yourself God."*
>
> (John 10:31–33)

Their reaction against Jesus' ministry, as well as the proper reaction to Him, are summed up in this statement from John the apostle:

> *He was in the world, and the world was made through Him, and the world did not know Him. He came to His own, and His own did not receive Him. But as many as received Him, to them He gave the right to become children of God, to those who believe in His name.* (John 1:10–12)

Don't attempt to "kill" your blessing when it comes. Never allow yourself to put limits on God by bringing Him down to the level of humankind. He is God, and with Him all things are possible. (See Matthew 19:26.) The Jews sought to stone Jesus for so-called blasphemy when, in fact, they were the ones who were blaspheming against Him. They even accused Jesus of having a demon. (See John 10:20.) The One who had been casting out demons was now being maligned and accused of being possessed. This is why Jesus responded,

> *If I do not do the works of My Father, do not believe Me; but if I do, though you do not believe Me, believe the works, that you may know and believe that the Father is in Me, and I in Him.* (John 10:37–38)

Today, people are still rejecting Jesus and attempting to "stone" Him. Our contemporary method of stoning Jesus seems to be via the media. Anything that remotely suggests the name of Jesus is often attacked immediately. Yet the life and works of Jesus speak for themselves. How do we react to Him? We are responsible for our own responses to His work in our lives. Let's not "stone" Him with doubt and unbelief while He is attempting to bless us with the answers that we need.

The second incident from Jesus' life took place after His arrest:

> *Now Jesus stood before the governor. And the governor asked Him, saying, "Are You the King of the Jews?" Jesus said to him, "It is as you say." And while He was being accused by the chief priests and elders, He answered nothing. Then Pilate said to Him, "Do You not hear how many things they testify against You?" But He answered him not one word, so that the governor marveled greatly.*
>
> (Matthew 27:11–14)

Perhaps the most monumental rejection of Jesus is depicted in the various incidents that led up to Jesus' death. The religious and political leaders who condemned Him never acknowledged who He really was. Throughout all these Scriptures, one thing remains clear: Jesus never argued. He simply stated the facts and went about doing His Father's business.

Note that He never denied who He was to save Himself, but He also never allowed the people's ignorance to prevent Him from blessing them. Instead, it was their rejection of Him that, in many instances, caused them to miss out on His blessing and miraculous works. (See Mark 6:1–6.)

You will never receive the benefits of prayer by constantly giving up on the things of God. When you give up on God, you are ultimately giving up on yourself. For without Him, you are helpless to meet the real needs in your life and to fight the demonic attacks that come against you, as well as the distractions that seek to hinder your prayers.

Are You Ready for Answered Prayer?

The Word of God is just as alive today as it has ever been, but our reluctance to believe it often gets in the way of our receiving. When children go to their parents seeking to be given something, they want to know only one thing: "Can I have it? Yes or no?" Once a parent replies, "Yes," the kids rarely stick around to ask, "How are you going to give it to me?" They are so excited that the parent has said "yes" that the "how?" is of little or no relevance. In a sense, this is the attitude that we should have with God. We must not take His blessings for granted. Yet we must truly trust Him by believing that He knows what He is doing and that He always has our best interests at heart. Unless parents consistently break their promises, their children will naturally have faith in them to do what they say they're going to do. God is the ultimate Promise Keeper:

> *The entirety of Your word is truth, and every one of Your righteous judgments endures forever.* (Psalm 119:160)

> *His divine power has given to us all things that pertain to life and godliness, through the knowledge of Him who called us by glory and virtue, by which have been given to us exceedingly great and precious promises, that through these you may be partakers of the divine nature.*
> (2 Peter 1:3–4)

> *Let us hold fast the confession of our hope without wavering, for He who promised is faithful.* (Hebrews 10:23)

If God has said that He is going to do something, we must trust and believe that His Word will never fail.

> [Be] *confident of this very thing, that He who has begun a good work in you will*

complete it until the day of Jesus Christ.
(Philippians 1:6)

Confidence leaves no room for doubt, which means that you should not waver in believing that God will do exactly what He has promised.

God doesn't want you to get discouraged in prayer. He wants to answer your requests and cries. Continue to commune with Him, learn to know Him and His ways, obey His Word, and watch how He works in your life.

Chapter 3

Seeking Answers in False Gods

Some Christians unknowingly hinder the call of God upon their lives by seeking answers to life's questions from evil sources. Not long ago, it was a foreign and unpopular concept in America to think of people, especially those in a society with a Judeo-Christian heritage, looking to the stars for guidance. Today, however, because of the mass acceptance of depictions of the paranormal, the occult, and Eastern religions in the popular media, many people have been wooed by the idea that perhaps there are alternative routes to get to God—routes that violate and defy His teachings.

Looking to "Signs" rather than to God

One of the practices that has enthralled many people today—even Christians—is "sign-seeking" through psychic phenomena and the "secrets of the Zodiac." The devil has unfortunately succeeded in convincing many of us that these things are either harmless fun and do not infringe upon our relationship with God, or that they are actually compatible with Christianity. He knows that as more of us find so-called truth while seeking sources other than God, we will continue to be drawn away from Him and enticed further into the kingdom of darkness and deceptive practices. Yet these practices endanger our souls and prompt the anger of God.

We must never seek signs to avoid a true relationship with our Creator and Father. When the Pharisees sought a sign from Jesus to prove who He was, He immediately responded, *"An evil and adulterous generation seeks after a sign, and no sign will be given to it except the sign of the prophet Jonah* [Jesus' resurrection on the third day]" (Matthew 12:39). The Pharisees were more interested in seeking signs than in seeking God Himself. They were polluted by their narcissism and wanted God to cooperate with them in this erroneous practice.

One practice related to sign seeking is reading one's horoscope. The word horoscope is derived from the Greek words *hora*, meaning "hour," and *skopos*, meaning "watching—as it relates to the hour of one's birth."[2] Horoscopes are a means of divining information about an individual based

[2] Online Etymology Dictionary, http://www.etymonline.com/index.php?search=horoscope (accessed May 6, 2008).

upon the interpretations of astrology and celestial influences. According to the beliefs that derive from astrology, each individual's behavior and personality is governed by one of the twelve signs of the zodiac.

After Bishop Bloomer did a teaching on the ungodly nature of astrology, people from around the United States began writing to him to reveal that they had become involved in such things as reading horoscopes and tarot cards, seeking the advice of psychics, experimenting with demonic rituals, and so forth. Many of them were Christians who, after seeking God over a period of time, felt that they had not adequately received an answer from Him. Concluding that their prayers were ineffective, they made the decision to "seek God" through alternative means. Although something that indicated the evil nature of their activities tugged at their spirits, they ignored it because of their urgent desire for a quick fix to life's challenges and trials.

God holds the future; if we trust in Christ, nothing will separate us from His love.

When they do not hear from God in what they consider a timely manner, or when they do hear from Him but do not receive the answer they feel they need, some people brush off their spirituality and seek after other "gods." This leads to many satanic entrapments from which people find themselves incapable of escaping.

ENGAGING IN ABOMINATIONS

There is no substitute for true prayer to the one true God. Today, many psychic mediums even use the name of God, but the Word of the Lord is very clear:

> *There shall not be found among you any one that maketh his son or his daughter to pass through the fire* ["*sacrifices his son or daughter*" NIV], *or that useth divination, or an observer of times, or an enchanter, or a witch, or a charmer, or a consulter with familiar spirits, or a wizard, or a necromancer. For all that do these things are an abomination unto the LORD: and because of these abominations the LORD thy God doth drive them out from before thee.*
>
> (Deuteronomy 18:10–12 KJV)

Demonic Rituals

Let's discuss a few of the practices that the Lord commanded should not be found among us. First, no one should engage in the abominable practice of sacrificing a son or daughter to Satan or any false god. While almost all Christians would protest they have nothing to do with such a terrible practice, God does not want us engaging in any strange or demonic rituals that invoke demons and familiar spirits. Sometimes, groups will attempt to convince you that what they're doing is in the name of God, when it has nothing to do with Him at all. Don't be deceived!

Divination

Second, divination is the ritual of trying to unravel future events by interpreting omens. We must be careful not to be alarmed by present circumstances or fearful of future events so that we engage in any form of divination. Again, the Pharisees sought signs as opposed to seeking God. That is why the Lord rebuked them. Why seek answers in omens when we serve an omniscient God who gives wisdom and understanding? An attempt to obtain information concerning the future through ungodly means jeopardizes one's spiritual stand with God. God holds the future, and if we are trusting in Christ, nothing will separate us from His presence and love.

> *The eternal God is your refuge, and underneath are the everlasting arms.*
>
> (Deuteronomy 33:27)

> *Who shall separate us from the love of Christ? Shall tribulation, or distress, or persecution, or famine, or nakedness, or peril, or sword? As it is written: "For Your sake we are killed all day long; we are accounted as sheep for the slaughter." Yet in all these things we are more than conquerors through Him who loved us. For I am persuaded that neither death nor life, nor angels nor principalities nor powers,* ***nor things present nor things to come****, nor height nor depth, nor any other created thing,* ***shall be able to separate us from the love of God*** *which is in Christ Jesus our Lord.*
>
> (Romans 8:35–39, emphasis added)

If God withholds any information from us, we can know that it is for our own good or it is not the right time to receive it. Our job is to continue to trust and serve in His name. Jesus told His disciples,

> *It is not for you to know times or seasons which the Father has put in His own authority. But you shall receive power when the Holy Spirit has come upon you; and you shall be witnesses to Me in Jerusalem, and in all Judea and Samaria, and to the end of the earth.* (Acts 1:7–8)

Witchcraft

Enchanters practice witchcraft by casting spells in their attempts to influence events. Some people don't want to wait for God's will and timing, so they take matters into their own hands. They want to be in control rather than yielding to God's control, and they go their own way and sometimes fall into the occult. The prophet Samuel told Saul, after he had disobeyed God,

> *Behold, to obey is better than sacrifice.... For rebellion is as the sin of witchcraft, and stubbornness is as iniquity and idolatry.* (1 Samuel 15:22–23)

The Bible warns us that self-will and rebellion against God are like witchcraft, and we must repent of them. We must stay away from the art of witchcraft. In his book *Witchcraft in the Pews,* Bishop Bloomer addressed the controversy about the topic of witchcraft:

> Many will suggest that witchcraft is simply the harmless worship of nature. They claim that both Christianity and witchcraft serve a higher power and that there is no significant difference between the two.
>
> To this, I must strongly disagree. As Christians, we must be very clear

concerning the source of the *power* we are serving.[3]

As God's Word, the Bible gives direction to believers and others who are seeking a genuine relationship with God. We must examine what people claim is "good" or "godly" in the light of the Word of God. Sometimes, an individual can seem to say the right thing while operating with the wrong spirit. For instance, the following occurred when the apostle Paul and other believers were ministering in Philippi:

> *Now it happened, as we went to prayer, that a certain slave girl possessed with a spirit of divination met us, who brought her masters much profit by fortune-telling. This girl followed Paul and us, and cried out, saying, "These men are the servants of the Most High God, who proclaim to us the way of salvation." And this she did for many days.* (Acts 16:16–18)

Paul was not pleased with this situation because he recognized that even though what the girl was saying was true, she was saying it with the wrong spirit and purpose. Eventually, Paul turned to her and rebuked the evil spirit that was controlling her: *"I command you in the name of*

[3] George G. Bloomer, *Witchcraft in the Pews* (New Kensington, PA: Whitaker House, 2008), 17.

Jesus Christ to come out of her.' And he came out that very hour" (Acts 16:18).

There are many dangers attached to dabbling in things from which the Lord has commanded us to abstain. In Joshua, when the Lord delivered the city of Jericho to the children of Israel, He gave them a warning: *"By all means abstain from the accursed things, lest you become accursed when you take of the accursed things, and make the camp of Israel a curse, and trouble it"* (Joshua 6:18).

We must examine what people claim is "good" in the light of God's Word.

When you have made a covenant with God and then begin taking on accursed things and habits, it not only affects your life, but it can also have detrimental effects on those around you. The Israelite Achan harbored *"accursed things"* in the camp, and because he did not heed the Lord's advice, *"the anger of the Lord burned against the children of Israel"* (Joshua 7:1). As a result, when they went to fight against Ai, they had to flee in defeat.

Unanswered prayers are not always a result of sin and transgressions, but our sin and disobedience can prompt God's anger and hinder us from obtaining victory over the ongoing battles that we face in life. Regardless of how tempting it might seem to employ alternate means of having our needs met, we should keep our focus on God, knowing that He is the Source, the One who holds all that we need. He says in Isaiah, *"There is none besides Me. I am the Lord, and there is no other"* (Isaiah 45:6).

God will give you answers for how to address the needs and concerns you face: sickness, family crises, broken marriages, financial and career guidance, and so forth. He is the answer. There is none other besides Him. His Spirit cannot be "conjured up" through ungodly rituals, by paying for His presence, or through demonic transactions that contradict His commandments.

Simon the sorcerer found out the hard way that the power of God cannot be bargained for or bought.

> *When Simon saw that through the laying on of the apostles' hands the Holy Spirit was given, he offered them money, saying, "Give me this power also, that anyone on whom I lay hands may receive the Holy Spirit." But Peter said to him, "Your money perish with you, because you thought that the gift of God could be purchased with money! You have neither part nor portion*

> *in this matter, for your heart is not right in the sight of God. Repent therefore of this your wickedness, and pray God if perhaps the thought of your heart may be forgiven you. For I see that you are poisoned by bitterness and bound by iniquity."*
>
> (Acts 8:18–23)

Simon had been accustomed to having people pay him for his gift of foretelling future events, but he soon found that his so-called gift (the familiar spirit that ruled Simon's sorcery) was nothing in comparison to the purity and power of the Spirit of God.

There is a wrong spirit behind the predictions that people receive from reading horoscopes and going to psychics and fortune-tellers. Many people are drawn into these things because of their seeming ability to deliver quick answers to puzzling questions that haunt us in life. Satan sprinkles just enough truth on his poison to get people to digest it.

Keep your focus on God, knowing that He is the Source, the One who holds all you need.

Psychic phenomena have become so prevalent and prominent because many people are experiencing comfort in demonic predictions disguised as

God's truth. Once Satan reels you in, the next stage is to make you dependent upon his voice instead of on God's guidance. Satan attempted this with Jesus after He had fasted for forty days and forty nights. He wanted Jesus to listen to him and bow to him instead of to the Father. (See Matthew 4:1–11.) The devil may use either blatant or subtle tools to obtain people's worship, but his objective remains the same: to lure you into heeding his voice, as he did to Eve in the garden of Eden. (See Genesis 3:1–19.)

RESULTS OF LOOKING TO FALSE SOURCES

Let's summarize the dangers of looking to psychic and demonic sources in order to receive help and direction.

Being Deceived

First, looking to psychic and demonic sources leads to being deceived. Many psychic and horoscope readings are not predictions at all; they are nothing more than humankind's ability to manipulate the psyche of those who are receiving the information. With God, however, you always know that what you are receiving is accurate. *"God is not a man, that He should lie"* (Numbers 23:19). Jesus prayed to the Father on behalf of His disciples and all who would believe in Him through their testimony, *"Sanctify them by Your truth. Your word is truth"* (John 17:17).

Becoming Paranoid

The second danger is living a paranoid life. Have you ever noticed how paranoid people often become after receiving a prediction about their lives? One young lady confessed that every day, when she woke up, even before praying to God, she would read her daily horoscope and rely upon it to lead her throughout the day. If it stated something such as "Beware of coworkers," she'd go to her job in a bad mood, just waiting for someone, anyone, to rub her the wrong way. She became so consumed with her daily readings that there was little room left in her life to consult God.

Paranoia is the opposite of the peace God gives us.

> *You will keep him in perfect peace, whose mind is stayed on You, because he trusts in You. Trust in the LORD forever, for in YAH, the LORD, is everlasting strength.*
>
> (Isaiah 26:3–4)

"Perfect peace" does not imply that your life will be void of troubles and trials. Rather, it means that your mind will be able to remain tranquil and free of oppression no matter what is going on in your life, because you are not trusting in your own abilities but in the strength of the Lord. When you experience trials, you don't

lose your temper at others or attack those involved in your problems. You look to God for His solutions.

Being Pulled into the Demonic

Third, if you dabble in the psychic arena and look to occult sources for guidance, you can easily be pulled further into the realm of the demonic. You have relinquished your trust in God to satanic forces that want to control you and your life. You will likely be drawn further into the false avenues, leading to increased deception and disconnection from God. You may unwillingly be influenced by evil spiritual beings that want to frustrate your true potential in God and destroy you. *"Your adversary the devil walks about like a roaring lion, seeking whom he may devour"* (1 Peter 5:8). You are jeopardizing your relationship with God and your salvation!

When you experience trials, look to God for His solutions.

Experiencing God's Absence and Anger

Finally, embracing the demonic creates a wall between you and God's holy presence. He still loves you, but you are out of fellowship with Him and are actually joining forces with His enemy.

Engaging in occult and demonic practices will ultimately bring God's anger against you and may also affect your descendants. You should never become involved in anything today that could rob you and your children of God's blessings tomorrow.

> *You shall have no other gods before Me.... For I, the LORD your God, am a jealous God, visiting the iniquity of the fathers upon the children to the third and fourth generations of those who hate Me, but showing mercy to thousands, to those who love Me and keep My commandments.*
> (Deuteronomy 5:7, 9–10)

Never replace trusting God with looking to the ideas of human beings or demonic spirits. As the psalmist wrote,

> *Whom have I in heaven but You? And there is none upon earth that I desire besides You. My flesh and my heart fail; but God is the strength of my heart and my portion forever. For indeed, those who are far from You shall perish; You have destroyed all those who desert You for harlotry. But it is good for me to draw near to God; I have put my trust in the Lord GOD, that I may declare all Your works.* (Psalm 73:25–28)

Chapter 4

Communing with the Father

One of the best ways to counteract confusion over prayer is to spend time with God and learn to discern His voice. Many years ago, when I was young in the Lord, I desired to seek the counsel of God. I would get my children off to school, read my Bible, and then pray. I would pray in English and then I would worship God in the Spirit. I remember so well how I would get on my face to pray. I still do that today. I would be so caught up in the Spirit, talking to the Lord and communing with Him, that I wouldn't even realize the hours that had passed and how long I had been in prayer.

During the day, I would wash the dishes, do the laundry, clean the floors, and take care of all the household chores, but I would constantly have my mind on the Lord. I remember thinking, *Well, Lord, is this a normal thing to do?* Then I said to myself, "Well, if God said to commune with Him and talk to Him, then this is normal." The Scripture says, *"Rejoice always, pray without ceasing, in everything give thanks; for this is the will of God in Christ Jesus for you"* (1 Thessalonians 5:16–18). (See also, for example, Exodus 25:21–22 and Matthew 6:5–7.) We can't verbally pray to God twenty-four hours a day, but we can make ourselves continually available to Him for prayer or service, and we can constantly keep in touch with His presence, acknowledging Him in all things. We are to have a lifestyle of open communication with God.

If you continue to trust in God, He will walk you through the uncertainties of life.

Communing continually with God while I worked proved to be a great way to balance my home and my family. Through this practice, He also taught me that He was to be first in my life. He was the One to whom I was to look for answers. He was the One to whom I was to look when I was going through crises. He was always there with me, and I learned to trust Him by communicating with Him.

Yes, I still failed at times, but I would go directly to God—my Daddy—by getting back on my knees and praying. Sometimes, when I was driving my car, the Spirit of the Lord would come over me, and I would just pull the car over and begin to pray, "Father, please guide me this day and lead my steps."

We all are in great need of the Father's guidance. As people wake up each morning all over the world, they do not know what is in store for them. We do not know what today holds, so we must hold on to God's hand. He has been with me through the death of one of my children, the death of my mother, and the death of my sister. He has always held my hand through the storms of life. The Father has talked to me and communed with me, giving me strength that I never knew I could have.

Through the difficulties and oppositions of life, we cannot let go of God's hand, because He is the only One who can lead us to safety. You may not be able to see what lies ahead, but if you continue to trust in God, He will walk you through the uncertainties of life. That is why you should never give up when the pressure seems as if it is too much to bear. Just "pull over" to a quiet place and ask God to lead the way.

Understanding Communion with God

From the beginning of time, God has desired to commune with humankind. The Bible indicates that God would walk with Adam in the cool of the evening; they would have special fellowship together. (See Genesis 3:8.) Every human being has (1) a physical body, which houses the spirit and soul; (2) a soul (mind, will, and emotions through which we reason, choose, and feel); and (3) a spirit.

God made us in His image (see Genesis 1:26), and *"God is Spirit"* (John 4:24). Your spirit is the essence of who you are, and it is through your spirit that you are meant to communicate directly with your heavenly Father. Yet, again, in order for us to communicate with God through our spirits, we must first be born again and have our spirits regenerated through Christ.

> *And if anyone does not have the Spirit of Christ, he does not belong to Christ. But if Christ is in you, your body is dead because of sin, yet your spirit is alive because of righteousness.* (Romans 8:9–10 NIV)

Obviously, people can pray to God before having their spirits regenerated since He hears their prayers for salvation and help. Yet truly communing with Him in the way He intends can occur only when our spirits are renewed and we have His own Spirit dwelling within us. The apostle Paul wrote,

> *And if the Spirit of him who raised Jesus from the dead is living in you, he who*

raised Christ from the dead will also give life to your mortal bodies through his Spirit, who lives in you....Those who are led by the Spirit of God are sons of God. For you did not receive a spirit that makes you a slave again to fear, but you received the Spirit of sonship. And by him we cry, "Abba, Father." The Spirit himself testifies with our spirit that we are God's children. (Romans 8:11, 14–16 NIV)

Paul also said,

I will pray with my spirit, but I will also pray with my mind; I will sing with my spirit, but I will also sing with my mind. (1 Corinthians 14:15 NIV)

We are further instructed to

pray in the Spirit on all occasions with all kinds of prayers and requests. With this in mind, be alert and always keep on praying for all the saints. (Ephesians 6:18 NIV)

Distractions to Communion with God

Since communing with God is so vital, we must learn how to recognize and deal with distractions that would keep us from developing a consistent prayer life.

Physical Distractions

While we should always take time to find a quiet place to talk to God, we should not allow a lack of quietness to keep us from fellowshipping with Him. Prayer can be accomplished anywhere and anytime. When you are not able to speak verbally to God, talking silently to Him can be just as effective. Whether you are jogging, sitting at your desk, waiting in the doctor's office, flying on an airplane, or even playing golf on a green, there are no barriers between you and God when it comes to prayer.

When you are not able to speak verbally to God, talking silently to Him can be just as effective.

All too often, we allow the constraints of ritualistic traditions to keep us from God when all He wants is our time and effort. You don't have to be in a church in order to pray. It doesn't matter if you stand or sit while speaking to Him. It doesn't require the burning of candles or seclusion. God will talk to you any time of the day or night. You should never be so busy in life that you ignore Him. Do not allow anyone or anything to keep you from God, for in Him lies the wisdom of life:

> *The fear of the LORD is the beginning of wisdom; a good understanding have all*

> *those who do His commandments.*
> (Psalm 111:10)

> *For wisdom is a defense as money is a defense, but the excellence of knowledge is that wisdom gives life to those who have it.* (Ecclesiastes 7:12)

> *He will be the sure foundation for your times, a rich store of salvation and wisdom and knowledge; the fear of the LORD is the key to this treasure.* (Isaiah 33:6 NIV)

We need to continually acknowledge God's presence and recognize that He welcomes our conversation with Him, no matter where we are. None of us knows the day or the hour when Jesus will return (see Matthew 25:13) or when we will die and go to be with God, so we cannot afford to put off communing with Him.

Demonic Distractions

Second, we must be aware that demonic distractions may come to hinder our prayers. I earnestly believe that the devil understands the significance and power of our communication with the Father. He attempts to keep us so busy and bogged down with our personal problems that we fail to take time to pray. He will use whatever it takes to get you to think about anything but God.

This explains why, often, the minute you go into prayer, the phone will ring, someone will knock at the door, or you will think of something that you have do "right away," although you've been putting it off for months.

Demons will try to cause disturbances and wreak havoc in your life so that you will focus your attention on these distractions and concerns. They will try to keep you from remaining diligent in prayer and in a state of faithfulness and obedience to God.

Give God the priority He deserves without allowing distractions to keep you from Him.

Please understand that your loved ones and friends who call you or stop by to see you when you are praying are not "the devil." Neither are the work tasks that distract you. Satan will use people and things in your life as pawns to keep you from approaching the King's throne. The devil knows that in order to get your attention, he has to use someone or something close to you. He may whisper to someone close to you, "Hurry up! Call her right now." I am not suggesting that you should shun your friends or responsibilities; rather, I'm stressing the need to have a balance in your life and to give God the priority

He deserves without allowing distractions to keep you from Him. Recognize that you need time alone with Him.

To build a closer relationship with God, sometimes you need to turn off the telephone and put a sign on your door that reads "Please Do Not Disturb." Take time to prepare yourself for some serious quality time with God. You can even make a prayer room in your home so that everyone knows not to bother you once the door is closed. Place pictures of your loved ones and others who need prayer before you as a point of contact. Because distance makes no difference in prayer, you can simply agree with them in your prayer room and call out their needs to God.

Results of Communing with the Father

What are some results of our communing with the Father? We (1) have oneness and unity with Him, (2) receive spiritual strength, (3) reflect God's light to others, (4) receive God's guidance, and (5) learn to discern His voice for ourselves and for ministering to others.

Oneness with God

One of the most remarkable characteristics of Jesus was His oneness with the Father:

I and My Father are one. (John 10:30)

He who has seen Me has seen the Father. (John 14:9)

A little while longer and the world will see Me no more, but you will see Me. Because I live, you will live also. At that day you will know that I am in My Father, and you in Me, and I in you. (John 14:19–20)

What is perhaps even more remarkable is that Jesus said we also are to live in oneness with God through Him.

If anyone loves Me, he will keep My word; and My Father will love him, and We will come to him and make Our home with him. (John 14:23)

That they all may be one, as You, Father, are in Me, and I in You; that they also may be one in Us, that the world may believe that You sent Me. (John 17:21)

And I have declared to them Your name, and will declare it, that the love with which You loved Me may be in them, and I in them. (John 17:26)

Jesus' oneness with the Father was so complete that They were working in total unity. *"Most assuredly, I say to you, the Son can do nothing of Himself, but what He sees the Father do; for whatever He does, the Son also does in like manner"* (John 5:19). The Scriptures say that Jesus would take time to go off by Himself to pray to God and seek His will. (See, for example, Matthew 14:23; Mark 1:35; Luke 6:12; 9:28.) He was of one mind and heart with the Father. This is the same relationship God desires to have with us, and for which He made provision through the life, death, and resurrection of Jesus.

> *This is the covenant that I will make with the house of Israel after those days, says the* L*ORD*: *I will put My laws in their mind and write them on their hearts; and I will be their God, and they shall be My people.*
> (Hebrews 8:10)

Spiritually, we are sitting—even now—in "heavenly places" with Christ:

> *But God, who is rich in mercy, because of His great love with which He loved us, even when we were dead in trespasses, made us alive together with Christ (by grace you have been saved), and raised us up together, and made us sit together in the heavenly places in Christ Jesus, that in the ages to come He might show the*

> *exceeding riches of His grace in His kindness toward us in Christ Jesus.*
>
> (Ephesians 2:4–7)

One day, we will see God face-to-face (see 1 Corinthians 13:12), and God will live among human beings.

> *And I heard a loud voice from heaven saying, "Behold, the tabernacle of God is with men, and He will dwell with them, and they shall be His people. God Himself will be with them and be their God."*
>
> (Revelation 21:3)

Even now, God desires a close relationship with us, so that His thoughts will become our thoughts and His ways will become our ways. (See Isaiah 55:6–9.) As you seek oneness with the Father, He will welcome you into His presence and admonish, "Come, let us walk this road of life together."

Think about how sinners get saved. They reach out to God in Jesus' name, acknowledging who He is, repenting of their sins, and calling upon Him for salvation and help. You continue your relationship with Him in a similar way. You reach out to Him, acknowledging His greatness; you receive forgiveness for any sin you have committed so you may be in clear fellowship with Him; and you call upon Him for your needs and requests.

Spiritual Strength

Receiving strength is another result of communing with the Father. After I have confessed my sins and poured out all my thoughts to God, I feel clean and renewed. Prayer can refresh us spiritually, mentally, emotionally, and physically. When Nehemiah was harassed by his enemies, he prayed, *"Now therefore, O God, strengthen my hands"* (Nehemiah 6:9). Jesus received spiritual strength through an angel after earnestly praying to the Father in the garden of Gethsemane.

> *He withdrew about a stone's throw beyond* [Peter, James, and John], *knelt down and prayed, "Father, if you are willing, take this cup from me; yet not my will, but yours be done." An angel from heaven appeared to him and strengthened him.*
>
> (Luke 22:41–43 NIV)

Paul prayed that the Ephesians would experience spiritual strength:

> *I pray that out of his glorious riches he may strengthen you with power through his Spirit in your inner being, so that Christ may dwell in your hearts through faith.* (Ephesians 3:16–17 NIV)

Prayer keeps us close to God and spiritually strong.

Reflecting God's Light to Others

When we commune with the Father, we are better able to reflect His light and mercy in the world. A lack of communication with God prevents us from developing an effective prayer life, and an ineffective prayer life results in a lifestyle of spiritual mediocrity. God can be visible to others through you only when you are communing with Him and are in harmony with His Spirit. Jesus said, *"Let your light so shine before men, that they may see your good works and glorify your Father in heaven"* (Matthew 5:16). As you develop a secret prayer life with God, it will be reflected in your public life.

> *But you, when you pray, go into your room, and when you have shut your door, pray to your Father who is in the secret place; and your Father who sees in secret will reward you openly.* (Matthew 6:6)

Receiving God's Guidance

Fourth, an active prayer life of communion with God will enable you to receive God's guidance. Prayer is the key to unlocking the heart of God. It's in prayer that God will reveal to you many things because He loves and cares for you. He will begin to open up His Word to you and may even show you visions. As I have communed with God and spent intimate time with Him, I have received visions in which I have seen the Word in action. Like a movie revealing its plot to anxious viewers, I have seen how the Lord delivers people through prayer.

All too often, people tirelessly seek out alternatives to life's issues instead of going to God first. Many of our dilemmas could be drastically reduced if we went to God, communed with Him, and asked this simple question: "Lord, what would You have me do in this situation?"

Learning to Discern His Voice

Fifth, communing with the Father helps us to learn to discern His voice. It is vital to listen to Him as you express your worship, concerns, and requests. You must give Him "space" to talk to you. When you call or visit with a friend, it's very frustrating to be the only one doing the talking. In order to have a conversation, there must be interaction between both parties. The same is true in your relationship with God the Father. Prayer must be a two-way conversation. The more you pray and listen for His voice so that you can obey it, the more you will see things in your life begin to change.

God will speak to you in His timing. We are not to ask Him to speak to us and then believe anything that pops into our heads is from Him. We are to use discernment in determining His voice. Here are some keys to help you:

- God will not tell you to do anything that contradicts His Word. He doesn't argue when it comes to His Word. It is what it is, and there are no compromises.
- God's Word is pure. *"Every word of God is pure; He is a shield to those who put their trust in Him. Do not add to His words, lest He rebuke you, and you be found a liar"* (Proverbs 30:5–6).
- When we put our trust in God and His pure Word, He becomes our shield. Psalm 91:4 reminds us, *"His truth shall be your shield and buckler."* Since God's Word is pure, we are not to add to what He says, nor are we to take away from it. His Word is already perfect; to add to it or take away from it contaminates its authenticity and robs us and others of its power.
- When God speaks, He makes it easy for you to hear Him. When He is silent, sometimes that simply means to "wait."
- God will not tell you to do anything that jeopardizes the spiritual or physical lives of others.

- Your conscience is a gift from God—one that you should not ignore.

The more you commune with God, the easier it becomes to know when He is speaking. God began to train me over the years to step out and obey His voice when He speaks. I would be in a service about to preach on hell when, all of a sudden, God would begin speaking to me about things that people in the congregation were going through.

The more you commune with God, the easier it becomes to know when He is speaking.

For instance, the Lord would say, "Write these things down." So I'd write as God revealed healings that were about to take place and other blessings that He wanted to give to the congregation. As I got up to speak, I would share with the people what God had shown me. I would say something like, "God says that there are people who have migraine headaches. He says that some of them are nerve-related and others are related to stress. There is pressure in the head that is being caused by a spirit of infirmity—an attack of the enemy. I'm going to ask you to come up here if you have a migraine headache, because whoever you are, God wants to heal you today!"

People would come out of the audience to the altar for prayer—sometimes ten people, and on other occasions fifty or one hundred. I would question them, "How long have you had this affliction, this headache?"

One would say, "All my life," others would answer, "Only a few months," and still others, "A few days." And some would say, "It comes and goes."

I would close my eyes and begin to pray. Sometimes, I would see a dark, black band around their heads, and the Lord would reveal to me that it was an attack of the enemy and for me to "break that band, in the name of Jesus."

If we will walk close to God, He will fulfill His will in our lives.

I would begin doing spiritual warfare for the person, saying, "In Jesus' name, I break this band and command migraine headaches to be loosed and let this person go!" I would actually see angels come and break that demonic stronghold, and it would disappear into the air. Then the Lord would have me pray for restoration and healing. I would see the Word of God come in and begin to touch the person's head and bless him or her. As God's glory seemed to come all over the person, I knew the Lord was bringing healing.

Then I would pray for the next person, and I would see the bone structure and pressure on the nerves and the spine. The Lord would instruct me on how to pray for that person, and as I obeyed, He would perform a creative miracle of healing in His name. It's different all the time, and I just praise God for that because, in obeying God, I've learned a very valuable lesson that I would like to share with you: you have to trust God and flow with His Holy Spirit in whatever capacity He has given you.

Concerning the gifts of God, the book of 1 Corinthians reveals that there are different manifestations of His healing power. Note that gifts of healings is in the plural:

> *But the manifestation of the Spirit is given to each one for the profit of all: for to one is given the word of wisdom through the Spirit, to another the word of knowledge through the same Spirit, to another faith by the same Spirit, to another* ***gifts of healings*** *by the same Spirit, to another the working of miracles, to another prophecy, to another discerning of spirits, to another different kinds of tongues, to another the interpretation of tongues. But one and the same Spirit works all these things, distributing to each one*

> *individually as He wills.*
> (1 Corinthians 12:7–11, emphasis added)

Just as God heals in different ways, He uses people in different ways through a variety of gifts:

> *There are diversities of gifts, but the same Spirit. There are differences of ministries, but the same Lord. And there are diversities of activities, but it is the same God who works all in all.* (1 Corinthians 12:4–6)

There are different gifts, but they are all operated by the same God. That means that regardless of who possesses the gift, if that person is yielded to God's Spirit, the gift will fulfill the Lord's purpose. It is not our wills that manifest the gifts. Our prayer should be, "Lord, Your will be done."

There is one God who uses many vessels to carry out His various assignments *"for the profit of all"* (1 Corinthians 12:7). Almighty God works in ways beyond our reason, beyond our abilities, but if we walk close to Him and listen to Him, He will work through us to fulfill His will in our lives and in others' lives.

> *"For My thoughts are not your thoughts, nor are your ways My ways," says the*

> *Lord. "For as the heavens are higher than the earth, so are My ways higher than your ways, and My thoughts than your thoughts."* (Isaiah 55:8–9)

Accustomed to Communing

God wants us to become accustomed to communing with Him. There is an abundance of untapped revelation and knowledge that He wants to give to those who will listen to His voice and obey His commands. Have you ever come up with an idea and later asked yourself, *Where did that come from?* Or have you ever given advice to someone who was in the midst of a severe crisis and then thought later, *That was some great advice.* Even when we don't realize it, God is leading and guiding us. This becomes more apparent as we continually step out in faith and trust Him.

The more time you spend with God, the more prepared you become to minister a word of encouragement to others.

> *I charge you therefore before God and the Lord Jesus Christ,...preach the word! Be ready in season and out of season. Convince, rebuke, exhort, with all longsuffering and teaching.* (2 Timothy 4:1–2)

This passage reminds us to be prepared not only when things are going well, but also during seasons of "drought" so that we still have an anointed word to meet the need. You never know when God is going to use you to be a blessing to someone else, so always be ready to make yourself available to Him.

Prayer, therefore, gives us the opportunity to commune with God, to offer Him our requests, and to minister to others. As we have seen, He receives every prayer, sifts through it, answers it, and begins manifesting portions of it on earth in His timing. Once you grasp hold of that all-important fact, you will become less likely to *"grow weary while doing good"* (Galatians 6:9), and you will continue to enjoy fellowship with the Lord. Your attitude will become, *I have submitted it to God in prayer. I will make myself available to listen to His voice, and I know that He will work out all things for my good.* (See Romans 8:28.)

Chapter 5

Lord, Help Me to Pray!

Communing with God involves understanding how God desires us to come to Him and in what ways He wants us to pray. Three passages of Scripture will help us to gain this understanding, one from the Old Testament and two from the New Testament. We will begin with a passage that is familiar to many Christians from the book of 2 Chronicles. It teaches how God's people are to approach Him and to live their lives if they want Him to hear them.

Requirements for Having God Hear

> *If My people who are called by My name will humble themselves, and pray and seek My face, and turn from their wicked ways, then I will hear from heaven, and will forgive their sin and heal their land.*
> (2 Chronicles 7:14)

Second Chronicles 7:14 outlines four requirements for God's people if they want to be in right standing with Him and receive His help. They are to (1) humble themselves, (2) pray, (3) seek God's face, and (4) turn from their sinful ways.

Humble Yourself

James 4:10 says, *"Humble yourselves in the sight of the Lord, and He will lift you up."* Unless we are humble, we will not bow to God or seek Him for assistance. The haughtiness of our nature causes us to rely upon human ingenuity and skill, which are limited in power and ability.

> *Even the youths shall faint and be weary, and the young men shall utterly fall, but those who wait on the Lord shall renew their strength.* (Isaiah 40:30–31)

In contrast, God's power is unlimited. Regardless of what hindrances we run into along the way, *"with God all things are possible"* (Matthew 19:26). Moreover, we know that God works all things together for the good of those who love Him and are *"called according to His purpose"* (Romans 8:28).

Many times, we mistakenly equate "humility" with a type of weak, shameful, or dishonorable demeanor. On the contrary, humility is a position of respect. It is respecting yourself enough to honor the sovereignty of God by stepping aside and allowing Him to lead the way. As you allow yourself to be led by God, you open yourself to receive His revelatory knowledge—knowledge that can be attained only through worshipping Him and availing yourself of His voice. Proverbs 15:33 says, *"The fear of the Lord is the instruction of wisdom, and before honor is humility."* Before you can receive the wisdom of God, you must first listen.

Prayer keeps you grounded when winds of doubt begin to blow upon your faith.

After you listen and receive, you must begin to apply the wisdom that God has given. Only then can honor be bestowed on your behalf.

Pray

After you have humbled yourself and received God's knowledge and wisdom, you must pray to God for His strength and guidance to remain on track. Prayer is essential for maintaining one's focus when earnestly seeking to fulfill the call of God. Many times, as soon as we announce what God is about to do in our lives, the attacks of the devil come immediately to discount the word we have spoken based on God's promises. This is not coincidental, for Jesus said,

> *The sower sows the word. And these are the ones by the wayside where the word is sown. When they hear, Satan comes immediately and takes away the word that was sown in their hearts.* (Mark 4:14–15)

Whenever you speak a word affirming the will of God or His forthcoming blessings, expect the devil to come immediately to stir up disbelief. Not only does he want you to question the validity of the word that was spoken, but he also wants to invoke his doubting spirit upon all who heard you speak it. Prayer causes you to remain rooted and grounded when the satanic winds of doubt and unbelief begin to blow upon your faith. Remind yourself, "I know what God spoke, and regardless of what it looks like in the natural, I will not be moved!" Then pray, "God, I receive Your divine guidance and patiently wait for the physical manifestation of what You have already accomplished in the spiritual realm."

Seek God's Face

Seeking the face of God means, in part, remaining open to receive His voice of instruction and command, even when we least expect it. It also means to commune with Him regularly and diligently read His Word. As we seek Him, not only will He send help to meet our needs, but He will also give us supernatural discernment to protect us from those desiring to prey upon our vulnerabilities in times of need. *"Beware of false prophets, who come to you in sheep's clothing, but inwardly they are ravenous wolves"* (Matthew 7:15). When God speaks, you never have to worry about His having any bad motives or intentions. His divine love always desires the best for you.

> *For I know the thoughts that I think toward you, says the LORD, thoughts of peace and not of evil, to give you a future and a hope. Then you will call upon Me and go and pray to Me, and I will listen to you. And you will seek Me and find Me, when you search for Me with all your heart.*
> (Jeremiah 29:11–13)

Turn from Sinful Ways

Obviously, if we want God to move on our behalf in answer to prayer, we must turn away from all known sin and pursue the character and ways of God. We can also ask Him to reveal sin we are unaware of so we can repent of that, as well.

> *Who can discern his errors? Forgive my hidden faults. Keep your servant also from willful sins; may they not rule over me. Then will I be blameless, innocent of great transgression.* (Psalm 19:12–13 NIV)

In the next chapter, we will discuss hindrances to prayer that may fall under either "willful sins" or "hidden sins," but which need to be dealt with for effective prayer. *"The effective, fervent prayer of a righteous man avails much"* (James 5:16).

As you fulfill these four requirements—humbling yourself, praying, seeking the face of God, and turning from your sinful ways—He promises to hear your prayers and meet your needs: "I will forgive your sin and heal your land." (See 2 Chronicles 7:14.)

The above Scripture passage outlines our approach to God, and the following passages show us how we are to pray.

Jesus Taught the Way to Pray

Those who are unaccustomed to talking with God often ask, "How do you pray?" Even the disciples who lived and ministered with Jesus struggled to understand prayer, but they recognized that Jesus had the kind of prayer life they wanted. They asked Him to teach them how to pray, so Jesus took time to instruct them in what to do and what not to do when speaking to the heavenly Father. Today, we can follow these same guidelines as outlined in Jesus' teaching from the sixth chapter of Matthew:

> *When you pray, you shall not be like the hypocrites. For they love to pray standing in the synagogues and on the corners of the streets, that they may be seen by men. Assuredly, I say to you, they have their reward. But you, when you pray, go into your room, and when you have shut your door, pray to your Father who is in the secret place; and your Father who sees in secret will reward you openly. And when you pray, do not use vain repetitions as the heathen do. For they think that they will be heard for their many words. Therefore do not be like them. For your Father knows the things you have need of before you ask Him.* (Matthew 6:5–8)

Dos and Don'ts for Prayer

Jesus taught that when we pray, we need to keep a pure heart and the right motives:

- *Do not* pray just to be seen by others.
- *Do not* use "vain repetitions."

Prayer is personal communication between you and God. When people pray to show off to others the depth of their "spirituality," their prayers are rendered ineffective. Hypocrites are those who say one thing but do another. This type of behavior is like the girl possessed with the spirit of divination who followed Paul around, whom we read about in Acts 16. She seemed to say all the right things, but she wasn't saying them for the right reasons or with the right spirit.

Those who find pleasure in trying to prove their supposed spiritual maturity never allow themselves the real pleasure of experiencing the purity of God's blessings, which can be revealed only by praying His will with a pure heart.

> *You do not have because you do not ask. You ask and do not receive, because you ask amiss, that you may spend it on your pleasures.* (James 4:2–3)

When we pray, therefore, we are not to worry about what others are doing or thinking, and we are not to show off.

God responds to the sincere hearts of those who have His interests in mind.

In addition, we are not to try to reach God by using fancy words or formulas for prayer. God sees the person behind the words and does not judge us based upon how eloquently we speak. Neither are we to ramble on without thinking about what we're saying. God responds to those whose hearts are sincere and who have His interests in mind. When God sent Samuel to anoint a new king of Israel from among the sons of Jesse, Samuel assumed the qualifications for kingship would be revealed in his physical stature. He was thinking from an earthly point of view. The Lord was swift to remind him, however, that He hadn't chosen a specific man to lead the people because of his outward appearance but because of the quality of his inner man. *"For the Lord does not see as man sees; for man looks at the outward appearance, but the Lord looks at the heart"* (1 Samuel 16:7).

- *Do* find a private place to retreat to in order to commune with God so that you will be less inclined to feel spiritual pride and seek glory for yourself in the eyes of others.
- *Do* acknowledge that the Father already knows what you need before you pray.

Again, praying to God with an earnest heart in private reaps its rewards in public. Jesus admonished the disciples to pray with the right intentions. He also taught them to trust in God's provision. God is aware of all your needs, so you must believe Him and trust Him to provide in His timing.

A Pattern for Effective Prayer

As we have discussed, many Christians make the mistake of giving up on God just before receiving their miracles from Him. To keep this from happening to the disciples and to help them keep the correct perspective and focus, Jesus gave them the following pattern for effective prayer and remaining in the Father's will:

> *In this manner, therefore, pray: Our Father in heaven, hallowed be Your name. Your kingdom come. Your will be done on earth as it is in heaven. Give us this day our daily bread. And forgive us our debts, as we forgive our debtors. And do not lead us into temptation, but deliver us from the evil one. For Yours is the kingdom and the power and the glory forever. Amen.*
>
> (Matthew 6:9–13)

Jesus taught His disciples to begin prayer by showing honor and respect to the Father. *"Our Father in heaven, hallowed be Your name"* (verse 9). Always take time to worship God before making your requests. Throughout the Word of God, true worship brings the presence and power of the Lord. When we worship God, we are ushered into His presence. First Chronicles 16:27 says, *"Glory and honour are in his presence; strength and gladness are in his place"* (1 Chronicles 16:27 KJV). Wholehearted worshippers are encompassed by God's glory. In God's holy presence, there is no room for pride or selfishness.

"Your kingdom come. Your will be done on earth as it is in heaven" (Matthew 6:10). Praying the will of God means asking that what already has been done in heaven will be physically manifested upon the earth. You must have the same mind-set that Jesus had: *"Not My will, but Yours, be done"* (Luke 22:42). Having this mind-set comes from developing a level of trust and faith in God that affirms, Whatever His will is for my life, it is right.

Many times, we are hesitant to ask for God's will because it means giving up our personal "control." It means totally depending upon Him for direction. Most importantly, it means giving up the things that our fleshly nature loves in order to discover what the Spirit has in store for us instead. We always need to pray according to the will of God. Again, many prayers may not be answered because they are prayed with selfish objectives or sinful intentions.

Genesis 11:1 says that early in human history, *"the whole earth had one language and one speech."* Yet the people attempted to build a tower whose top would reach into heaven, just to build up their own pride.

> *Come, let us build ourselves a city, and a tower whose top is in the heavens; let us*

> *make a name for ourselves, lest we be scattered abroad over the face of the whole earth.* (Genesis 11:4)

Because the people sought their own selfish purposes, God stepped in and confused their language so that they would not understand one another's speech. This shut down their building program. It is always better to consult God first rather than to risk wasting time building something that goes against His will.

Pray to keep in the right mind-set when you face something wrong that seems desirable.

"Give us this day our daily bread" (Matthew 6:11). Regardless of what hardships may befall you, ask God to continue meeting your daily sufficiency. He has promised that as we are generous and give to others out of love for Him, He will supply everything we need. *"And my God shall supply all your need according to His riches in glory by Christ Jesus"* (Philippians 4:19).

Praying for God to give you daily sustenance not only puts Him in remembrance of His Word, but also paves the way for His will to continue being done in your life. The widow in 1 Kings 17 witnessed God's sustaining power firsthand after declaring to the prophet Elisha that she was gathering the last meal for herself and her son and preparing to die. Elisha prophesied to her that her provisions would not run out, and *"the bin of flour was not used up, nor did the jar of oil run dry, according to the word of the Lord which He spoke by Elijah"* (1 Kings 17:16).

"And forgive us our debts, as we forgive our debtors" (Matthew 6:12). How can we expect to receive forgiveness from others when we refuse to operate in forgiveness ourselves? We will look at this important concept again in the next chapter. Harboring unforgiveness is a canker that eats at the very essence of your spiritual power and favor with God. In Matthew 18:23–35, Jesus told the story of a servant who was forgiven a huge debt by his master, the king, but did not apply that same mercy and forgiveness to his fellow servant. Therefore, the forgiveness that the king had bestowed upon him was revoked. When we refuse to forgive others of their trespasses, our heavenly Father will also refuse to forgive us.

> *For if you forgive men their trespasses, your heavenly Father will also forgive you. But if you do not forgive men their trespasses, neither will your Father forgive your trespasses.* (Matthew 6:14–15)

"And do not lead us into temptation, but deliver us from the evil one" (verse 13). Don't ever become so comfortable in your salvation that you feel you can no longer be tempted. Many people have found themselves entangled in a world of deceit due to such self-deception. As much as the devil is warring against our spirits, our greatest battles are within ourselves. The strength of temptation's grip comes from our own desires.

> *Let no one say when he is tempted, "I am tempted by God"; for God cannot be tempted by evil, nor does He Himself tempt anyone. But each one is tempted when he is drawn away by his own desires and enticed. Then, when desire has conceived, it gives birth to sin; and sin, when it is full-grown, brings forth death. Do not be deceived, my beloved brethren.*
>
> (James 1:13–16)

Pray that God will keep you in the right spiritual mind-set when you are presented with something that is wrong but seems desirable.

"For Yours is the kingdom and the power and the glory forever. Amen" (Matthew 6:13). Jesus' model prayer begins and ends with honoring the Father and affirming His kingdom. Earlier in the prayer, Jesus taught us to pray, *"**Your** kingdom*

come. ***Your*** *will be done on earth as it is in heaven"* (verse 10, emphasis added). We must always remember that the kingdom belongs to God and give Him the honor that He is due.

Keeping a Prayerful Attitude

The final passage of Scripture, from 1 Thessalonians, helps us to understand how to keep an ongoing prayerful mind-set. The apostle Paul wrote,

> *Rejoice always, pray without ceasing, in everything give thanks; for this is the will of God in Christ Jesus for you. Do not quench the Spirit. Do not despise prophecies. Test all things; hold fast what is good. Abstain from every form of evil.*
> (1 Thessalonians 5:16–22)

"Rejoice Always"

Rejoice! We usually find it easy to rejoice when things are going well. Yet Paul said we are to rejoice always. Whenever you are facing something very challenging or even traumatic in your life, you can rejoice by thinking of something that God has delivered you from in the past, how your present situation could be much worse, or how God will use it for your good. *"We know that all things work together for good to those who love God, to those who are the called according to His purpose"* (Romans 8:28). As you think about these things, begin to give Him praise for His mercy and grace. When you feel too weak to pray, praise can be just as powerful as prayer itself. It refocuses your mind on the presence and power of God.

"Pray without Ceasing"

Praying when times are good prepares you to remain spiritually strong when things go awry. Again, "praying without ceasing" does not mean that you pray out loud twenty-four hours a day, but that you remain aware of God's presence and are in continual communion with Him, with an attitude of worship and openness to hear His voice.

Praying when times are good prepares you to remain strong when things go awry.

"In Everything Give Thanks"

Giving thanks to God in all circumstances changes one's whole perspective:

> *You have turned for me my mourning into dancing; You have put off my sackcloth and clothed me with gladness, to the end that my glory may sing praise to You and*

> *not be silent. O LORD my God, I will give thanks to You forever.* (Psalm 30:11–12)

While in some matters we need to discover what the will of God is for our lives, we can know that giving thanks is always His will: *"In everything give thanks; for* ***this is the will of God*** *in Christ Jesus for you"* (1 Thessalonians 5:18, emphasis added). God loves it when we give Him thanks for the many blessings in our lives. We are acknowledging that

> *...every good gift and every perfect gift is from above, and comes down from the Father of lights, with whom there is no variation or shadow of turning.* (James 1:17)

Although God gives you the skills to perform certain tasks and to learn new things, *"you are not your own"* (1 Corinthians 6:19). Jesus said, *"Without Me you can do nothing"* (John 15:5). We must never forget the One who blesses even as we enjoy His blessings.

Honoring God in All Things

Paul's instructions in the rest of the passage show us how we can keep in a frame of mind for communion with God and receiving His wisdom and blessings. They help us to honor God in all things.

"Do not quench the Spirit" (1 Thessalonians 5:19). When God speaks to us through His Holy Spirit, we are to listen and obey with willing hearts. Don't ever ignore or reject what He is saying or suppress the fire of His anointing. Ephesians 4:30 says, *"Do not grieve the Holy Spirit of God, by whom you were sealed for the day of redemption."*

"Do not despise prophecies" (verse 20). When God's true word comes forth, we must heed and obey it.

We must learn to discern a person's motivation and not just what he is saying.

"Test all things; hold fast what is good" (verse 21). It is vital to be able to discern the voice of God. Just as we are to listen to a true word of God, we are to reject what does not come from Him. As we think we hear from God or as we hear others prophesy, we are to test these ideas and words by God's Word. Whatever is good, we are to *"hold fast."* Part of *"testing all things"* is discerning the spirit or motivation of a person and not just what that person is saying. The devil knows that he cannot always prevent the Word of God from going forth, so he will attempt to manipulate God's intended

purpose. Sometimes, you can find someone who is seemingly saying all the right things, but who has all the wrong intentions. He may be speaking out of pride or attempting to manipulate others. Two people with different motivations might say the same thing but prompt different effects—one that builds up or one that tears down or controls.

"Abstain from every form of evil" (verse 22). This verse reminds us once again that being in right relationship with God is essential for hearing His voice. We are to pursue His ways and seek His kingdom first.

Praying in the Name of Jesus

As we conclude this chapter, I want to emphasize one more significant element of prayer. Jesus taught us to pray to the Father in His name:

> *Most assuredly, I say to you, he who believes in Me, the works that I do he will do also; and greater works than these he will do, because I go to My Father. And whatever you ask in My name, that I will do, that the Father may be glorified in the Son. If you ask anything in My name, I will do it.* (John 14:12–14)

> *You did not choose Me, but I chose you and appointed you that you should go and bear fruit, and that your fruit should remain,*

> *that whatever you ask the Father in My name He may give you.* (John 15:16)

> *Most assuredly, I say to you, whatever you ask the Father in My name He will give you. Until now you have asked nothing in My name. Ask, and you will receive, that your joy may be full.* (John 16:23–24)

When we pray in the name of Jesus, we are praying in His authority. He desires that we receive answers to our prayers as we pray according to His will. Note that when we make requests in His name, we must pray in faith. Our lives also must be producing godly fruit in keeping with Jesus' nature and works. As we participate in God's work in the world, and as we pray to the Father in Jesus' name, we will receive what we have asked for and be filled with joy!

TOTAL DEPENDENCE ON GOD

These passages of Scripture give us great insights and instruction about how we are to approach God and in what ways He desires us to pray. As you follow these patterns in your prayer life, you will be able to commune with the Father and become valuable in prayer. In everything you do, maintain the right motives and lean on the Lord for His understanding. He receives your total dependence upon Him as worship.

Chapter 6

Overcoming Hindrances to Answered Prayer

In this chapter, we will explore significant hindrances that keep us out of fellowship with God and block our prayers from being answered. We will expand on some of the issues that we addressed in the last chapter regarding our approach to God in prayer.

Lack of a Pure Heart

The first hindrance is a lack of a pure heart. The Scripture says,

> *Who may ascend into the hill of the Lord? Or who may stand in His holy place? He who has clean hands and a pure heart, who has not lifted up his soul to an idol, nor sworn deceitfully. He shall receive blessing from the Lord, and righteousness from the God of his salvation.*
>
> (Psalm 24:3–5)

> *As obedient children, do not conform to the evil desires you had when you lived in ignorance. But just as he who called you is holy, so be holy in all you do; for it is written: "Be holy, because I am holy."*
>
> (1 Peter 1:14–16 NIV)

Having a pure heart does not mean that you will never struggle with sins and faults. First John 2:1–2 says, *"If anyone sins, we have an Advocate with the Father, Jesus Christ the righteous. And He Himself is the propitiation for our sins."* When we sin, we can pray to the Father for forgiveness according to Jesus' sacrifice on the cross for us. We can receive His help for our personal struggles. Going to God with a pure heart means that you have asked forgiveness for your sins and that your intentions are without guile or bitterness. *"Blessed is the man whose sin the Lord does not count against him and in whose spirit is no deceit"* (Psalm 32:2 NIV).

Dishonesty with God

A lack of a pure heart may be manifested in dishonesty with God. When people whom we love lie to us or try to deceive us, we say to ourselves, I wish they would just be real with me. You know that they are hiding things from you and covering up many things, but you still long for them to open up and be honest and true. God feels the same way about us.

Imagine you have an old-fashioned family doctor who has treated you for many years and is well acquainted with your physical and mental history. One day, you go to visit him or her and completely deny your years of documented medical history. Your doctor would certainly question your motives, but he or she might also question your mental soundness because you would be denying obvious realities. That is the equivalent of what we do when we go before God denying the sin and dark places in our lives.

A pure heart means you're forgiven and your intentions are without guile or bitterness.

The apostle John wrote,

> *If we say that we have fellowship with Him, and walk in darkness, we lie and do not practice the truth....If we say that we have no sin, we deceive ourselves, and the truth is not in us.* (1 John 1:6, 8)

The only way to be pure in heart is to tell God the truth: "God, here I am. I'm a liar. I'm a sinner. I did these wicked things, and I need You to set me free, in Jesus' name. I want to be real with You, and I want this sin and rebellion removed from me. Please forgive me and help me to live according to Your nature."

Covering Up Our True Nature

Jesus was referring to purity of heart when He rebuked the Pharisees in Matthew 23:26: *"Blind Pharisee, first cleanse the inside of the cup and dish, that the outside of them may be clean also."* Often, we attempt in vain to clean up on the outside in order to cover up what's really within. We want to look good to others, and even to God, but we cannot hide our true nature from Him.

> *The LORD searches all hearts and understands all the intent of the thoughts.*
> (1 Chronicles 28:9)

> *The lamp of the LORD searches the spirit of a man; it searches out his inmost being.*
> (Proverbs 20:27 NIV)

While washing His disciples' feet, Jesus taught about spiritual cleanliness and uncleanliness:

> *After that,* [Jesus] *poured water into a basin and began to wash the disciples' feet, and to wipe them with the towel with which He was girded. Then He came to*

Simon Peter. And Peter said to Him, "Lord, are You washing my feet?" Jesus answered and said to him, "What I am doing you do not understand now, but you will know after this." Peter said to Him, "You shall never wash my feet!" Jesus answered him, "If I do not wash you, you have no part with Me." Simon Peter said to Him, "Lord, not my feet only, but also my hands and my head!" Jesus said to him, "He who is bathed needs only to wash his feet, but is completely clean; and you are clean, but not all of you." For He knew who would betray Him; therefore He said, "You are not all clean." (John 13:5–11)

The Wycliffe Bible Commentary explains about this event,

> The act [of foot washing] was symbolic of inward cleansing....The washing of regeneration makes one clean in God's sight. This is symbolized in Christian baptism....Further cleansing of the spots of defilement is not a substitute for the initial cleansing but has meaning only in light of it.[4]

[4] Charles F. Pfeiffer and Everett F. Harrison, eds., *The Wycliffe Bible Commentary* (Chicago: Moody Press, 1962), 1102.

Jesus' sacrifice for us brings complete forgiveness and reconciliation with the Father. Yet we still need to receive ongoing forgiveness and cleansing for the sins we commit, so we may stay in fellowship with Him. First John 1:9 says, *"If we confess our sins, He is faithful and just to forgive us our sins and to cleanse us from all unrighteousness."*

Denying Our Real Condition

It's often very difficult for us to accept the truth concerning our spiritual condition and the uncleanliness that remains within, even when it's being pointed out to us by the All-knowing One—Jesus Himself. This was Peter's problem in Mark 14. When Jesus forewarned Peter about his denial of Him, Peter answered, *"'If I have to die with You, I will not deny You!'"* (Mark 14:31). The truth was revealed, however, after Jesus was arrested and taken away by the soldiers to the house of the high priest for trial. Peter attempted to go unnoticed in the courtyard of the house as he waited to see what would happen. After he was spotted and identified by a servant girl and others as one of Jesus' disciples, he responded angrily, *"I do not know this Man of whom you speak!"* (verse 71). Three times, Peter denied Jesus before the rooster crowed twice, just as Jesus had predicted. (See Mark 14:66–72.)

The Spirit Cleanses Us

All of Jesus' disciples either denied or abandoned Him (Judas went further and actually betrayed Him). Yet, after He rose from the dead, Jesus still gave the remaining eleven disciples the gift of the Holy Spirit. Why? He knew they needed the Holy Spirit within to help them overcome their sinful nature. Paul wrote,

> *But you were washed, but you were sanctified, but you were justified in the name of the Lord Jesus and by the Spirit of our God.* (1 Corinthians 6:11)

The Holy Spirit comes and cleanses us within, enabling us to become effective witnesses for Christ. Jesus told His disciples,

> *"Peace to you! As the Father has sent Me, I also send you." And when He had said this, He breathed on them, and said to them, "Receive the Holy Spirit."*
> (John 20:21–22)

> *But you shall receive power when the Holy Spirit has come upon you; and you shall be witnesses to Me.* (Acts 1:8)

People no longer see only you, but they also see God's Spirit, who is shining forth through your spirit.

God seeks true worshippers to worship Him in spirit and in truth:

> *The true worshipers will worship the Father in spirit and truth; for the Father is seeking such to worship Him. God is Spirit, and those who worship Him must worship in spirit and truth.* (John 4:23–24)

> *Blessed are the pure in heart, for they shall see God.* (Matthew 5:8)

Why hide your ailments from the One who is the ultimate Cure-all for everything? Don't cover them up; let Him remove them. Say, "Lord, I've been doing mere religious acts rather than developing a relationship with You. I am critical of others. I am jealous. I have hatred, bitterness, and unforgiveness in my heart. Deliver me from being controlled by the sinful nature and set me free, in Jesus' name." *"If you live according to the flesh you will die; but if by the Spirit you put to death the deeds of the body, you will live"* (Romans 8:13).

Through God's Spirit, we can forsake our sinful nature and take on God's nature.

Ask the Father to baptize you with His Holy Spirit, and I guarantee you that He will begin to clean you up and guide you. *"He will baptize you with the Holy Spirit and fire"* (Matthew 3:11; Luke 3:16). *"For our God is a consuming fire"* (Hebrews 12:29). The fire of God is a purifier; it purges and cleanses. The Holy Spirit is a gift for all of us. Through the work of God's Spirit in us, we can identify and forsake our sinful nature and instead take on God's nature.

> *Search me, O God, and know my heart; try me, and know my anxieties; and see if there is any wicked way in me, and lead me in the way everlasting.* (Psalm 139:23–24)

> *Be imitators of God as dear children.*
> (Ephesians 5:1)

When you have a pure heart, you can go to God and say, "Father, in the name of Jesus, bless my spouse and my children; I need You today," and God will hear you and begin dispatching His angels to answer your requests. Having a clear channel to God is so important because prayer is where God reveals the answers that you seek.

For years, I have been experiencing answers from God through prayer. Throughout my sixteen years of preaching the gospel of Jesus Christ, I have visited eighty-five nations, petitioning God and praying to Him for answers. As a result of these miraculous experiences, I have discovered an extremely important truth: when we seek God and are real with Him, honestly evaluating ourselves before Him and admitting the truth about ourselves, and when we ask for His help, He will lead us toward the right path and give us the answers that we need. When you begin to recognize this truth, seek God, and confess to Him your faults and problems, He is thrilled to receive you. Just as parents in the natural are proud when their children tell them the truth, so is our Father in heaven when we come to Him with sincerity and purity of heart.

Love, compassion, and justice are the heart of the Law.

> *Ask, and it will be given to you; seek, and you will find; knock, and it will be opened to you. For everyone who asks receives, and he who seeks finds, and to him who knocks it will be opened.*
>
> (Matthew 7:7–8)

IGNORING "WEIGHTIER MATTERS"

The book of Isaiah opens with a situation in which God refused to receive the prayers and sacrifices of the people of Israel. The reason? They were not truly seeking Him. Instead, they were observing religious rituals and presenting "meaningless offerings" while ignoring the needs of those around them—the orphans, the widows, and others in society who were not receiving justice. The Lord told them,

> *Stop bringing meaningless offerings! Your incense is detestable to me. New Moons, Sabbaths and convocations—I cannot bear your evil assemblies. Your New Moon festivals and your appointed feasts my soul hates. They have become a burden to me; I am weary of bearing them. When you spread out your hands in prayer, I will hide my eyes from you; even if you offer many prayers, I will not listen. Your hands are full of blood.* (Isaiah 1:13–15 NIV)

This passage is similar to Jesus' statement to the Pharisees, who focused on religious ritual rather than on love, compassion, and justice toward others, which is the heart of the Law.

> *Woe to you, scribes and Pharisees, hypocrites! For you pay tithe of mint and anise and cummin, and have neglected the weightier matters of the law: justice and mercy and faith. These you ought to have done, without leaving the others undone.*
> (Matthew 23:23)

As I will discuss more fully in the next chapter, God wants a sacrificed life—one that is submitted to Him and not focused merely on religious ritual or fulfilling our own selfish desires at the expense of others. When we engage in such empty practices, God will refuse our "sacrifices" and may even shut His ears to our prayers. The people of Israel angered God by seeking answers from Him without the intention of ceasing their evil ways. The Lord admonished them to stop their wickedness and instead to seek to do right by others.

> *"Wash yourselves, make yourselves clean; put away the evil of your doings from before My eyes. Cease to do evil, learn to do good; seek justice, rebuke the oppressor; defend the fatherless, plead for the widow. Come now, and let us reason together," says the* LORD, *"though your sins are like scarlet, they shall be as white as snow; though they are red like crimson, they shall be as wool."* (Isaiah 1:16–18)

ANGER AND UNFORGIVENESS

We discussed unforgiveness in the last chapter as we looked at Jesus' pattern for prayer. This area is so significant, however, that it is worth reviewing. Suppose you say to God, "Lord, You are just a prayer away, and I need You to answer my request," but in your heart and mind you have hatred toward your neighbor. Or perhaps you are holding on to bitterness because of what somebody did to you fifteen years ago. You're asking God to bless your husband, your children, and your neighbors, yet beneath all of that is a volcano of anger that has never been dealt with.

Weeks before I had the first visions of hell, God began to peel me like a banana, spiritually. He told me to forgive anyone toward whom I was holding unforgiveness. I could not receive the revelations from God without dealing with these things. This may seem inconsequential, but I even had to forgive a salesman from whom I had bought carpet. He had taken my money but never delivered the merchandise, and I was furious with him for quite some time. Yet it was affecting me spiritually.

If you are harboring unforgiveness, ask God to set you free in Jesus' name.

In addition, I was married to my first husband at the time, and I was very hard on him because I didn't understand him. For instance, sometimes he would have a beer with some of his friends, and instead of ministering to him in love, I would immediately attack him for it. I was so religious that I thought his actions would cause him to go to hell, so I'd open up the Bible and read Scriptures to him. He was a good man, but I had to learn about Jesus' mercy the hard way.

I'm not advocating drinking beer, but I mention this incident to point out the fact that people are working through all types of things in their lives, and as they're working through them, we don't need to hit them over the head with the Bible as I did with my ex-husband. (See 1 Peter 3:1–4.) God really had to prune me and cut things out of me because I was so religious. He really had to bring me back down to earth. After six months of preparation, God revealed to me, "I'm getting ready to take you on a journey, and when you go on that journey you must be totally sold out to Me. You have to understand that what I am going to show you is real."

But, again, I had to deal with the unforgiveness first.

Jesus said,

> *If you bring your gift to the altar, and there remember that your brother has something against you, leave your gift there before the altar, and go your way. First be reconciled to your brother, and then come and offer your gift.* (Matthew 5:23–24)

If you have bitterness or unforgiveness, tell the Father, and ask Him to set you free in the name of Jesus. Pray that His love will fill you and make you an overcomer in every facet of your life.

Pride

One of the most self-destructive hindrances is pride, which we noted in our discussion on how we are to approach God. The deadly deceit of pride limits your growth to what can be attained only through human ingenuity. It keeps you from admitting your mistakes, from taking the initiative to change them, and even from praying to God.

Pride was the demise of King Saul, and it has been the culprit behind the fall of many great men and women throughout history. After Saul's continued disobedience, the Spirit of the Lord departed from him. Seeing that God was silent and no longer answering him, Saul decided to seek out a medium to invoke the spirit of Samuel for guidance. (See 1 Samuel 28.) How might the story have ended differently had Saul repented before God with an earnest heart and then prayed for direction regarding the impending battle against the Philistines? Instead, Saul went into battle, and, after being wounded, committed suicide by falling upon his own sword. (See 1 Samuel 31.)

Pride says, "Don't admit your mistakes. It will cause you to be humiliated. Instead, continue to pretend as if you know what you are doing and allow nothing or no one to convince you to change." As you nod your head in agreement, pride gradually and subtly leads you to a tragic fall. (See Proverbs 16:18.) Proverbs 11:2 reveals that the very thing that prideful individuals are trying to avoid—shame—is what they eventually draw to themselves: *"When pride comes, then comes shame; but with the humble is wisdom"* (Proverbs 11:2). Pride leaves no room for growth, and it completely shuns wisdom. It has no patience and is quick to make decisions without first consulting God. The success of prayer depends on persistence and God's power. Giving up too quickly robs you of the experience of witnessing God's power and from enjoying His miraculous blessings.

Giving up too quickly on prayer robs you of witnessing God's power and blessings.

Lack of Spiritual Growth

A final hindrance is a lack of spiritual growth, which can come from spiritual apathy. It is as you grow in your understanding of God and His ways, apply His Word in faith, and obey Him that you will experience more power in prayer. It's very important to know that the power God wants to give you is the ability to be set free from sinful habits and from giving in to temptation, as well as to engage in spiritual warfare against the devil.

When you are born again and become a brand-new Christian, there are many things that God knows you are not ready to digest spiritually. A newborn has to be fed milk for quite a while. He has to be changed, held, loved, and encouraged. That's the way God is with you and me. He watches over us and protects us until we're renewed by His Word and can be mature workers for Him.

> *As newborn babes, desire the pure milk of the word, that you may grow thereby.*
>
> (1 Peter 2:2)

> *For everyone who partakes only of milk is unskilled in the word of righteousness, for he is a babe. But solid food belongs to those who are of full age, that is, those who by reason of use have their senses exercised to discern both good and evil.*
>
> (Hebrews 5:13–14)

Sometimes, it can seem like the more you grow in the Word of God, the more challenges you are forced to confront. This simply means that your spiritual growth is giving you the ability to retain the strong meat of the Word of God and a keen sense to discern both good and evil. James wrote, *"Count it all joy when you fall into various trials, knowing that the testing of your faith produces patience"* (James 1:2–3). It is also enabling you to grow even more. *"Every branch that bears fruit He prunes, that it may bear more fruit"* (John 15:2). Count it all joy!

Run to God in times of trouble instead of trying to hide from His presence.

God is almighty and holy, and only through Jesus Christ can you be reconciled to Him and be born again to eternal life. And only through this reconciliation can you grow spiritually and have an effective prayer life. This is why I want to ask once more, Have you been born again? If not, repent of your sins, receive forgiveness through the sacrifice of Jesus Christ on the cross for you, and begin living a life that is sold out for God. If you make mistakes, as everyone does, and if you fall, repent quickly in Jesus' name, get back up, and continue living your life for Him.

You must believe that Christ hung on the cross, shed His blood for you, and died on your behalf. When you ask Christ to come into your heart, save your soul, and forgive you of all your sins, you are born again through the Spirit of the living God. He washes you clean of your sins and makes you new. *"If anyone is in Christ, he is a new creation; old things have passed away; behold, all things have become new"* (2 Corinthians 5:17).

The Bible says,

> *God is not a man, that He should lie.... Has He said, and will He not do? Or has He spoken, and will He not make it good?*
> (Numbers 23:19)

God will do as He has promised. Therefore, new Christians and older Christians alike need to remember that when you enter into this covenant with God, you are a new creation in Christ. He will help you overcome the obstacles and temptations that you face. He will give you the milk of His Word, and then, as you become more mature, He will give you the solid food of the Word. As you read and study the Bible, and as you yield to the Holy Spirit's work in your life, you will become stronger and stronger in the Lord.

Again, you may make mistakes, but mistakes are part of the growth and learning process. As you grow, you're going to think you know it all when you don't really know anything. You're going to fall on your face many times. Yet it will be like a baby in the natural who falls and falls but continues to get back up until he becomes skilled at walking without stumbling.

God will either cushion the fall or let you learn from the bumps and bruises. But He will always dust you off and help you to rise back up again. Run to Him in times of trouble instead of trying to hide from His presence. Throughout our lives, we will face many troubles (see Job 14:1; John 16:33 NIV), but God is willing and able to deliver us from them all if we will only realize that He is indeed just a prayer away!

The Best Defense against Hindrances

The more you seek God's face and follow His instructions, the more you will see the manifestation of His deliverance and power working on your behalf. Yet you must remain diligent in your pursuit of Him and not give up. You must give God first place in your life so that it is not consumed with crises from which you have gained no revelation about how to escape.

The best defense against future outbreaks of the sinful nature and attacks of Satan is making time for God right now. Then, when these things arise, you already will have gained the revelation on how to defeat them from reading the Scriptures and praying. Instead of panicking, you will stand in boldness and confront them with the Word. If you do not learn to do this, they will continue to make you unstable in life and unfocused on the things of God.

Have you ever seen people who move from job to job? They are constantly starting a new job whenever conflict occurs because they have not mastered the art of conflict resolution. The same result can occur spiritually in your everyday life. When you fail to be trained in self-control and spiritual warfare through the Word and the power of prayer, you continually flee your battles instead of taking the time to win them. You find yourself constantly fighting a losing battle instead of engaging in the *"good fight of faith"* (1 Timothy 6:12).

When you continually try to work things out on your own without the assistance of God, you become frustrated, fatigued, and worn down. This may eventually cause you to give up. You begin to accept things in your character that you actually have the power to change. Or you just receive whatever the devil throws at you as your "plight in life." You accept mediocrity as a way of life instead of as one of many obstacles that you have the power to overcome through Christ.

Bishop Bloomer related the following:

> I had a dream one time where I was snatched away by the Holy Spirit and

taken into what I believe was heaven. I was standing on a balcony and the angel of the Lord said to me, "This is the *balcony of ages*." I looked over the top of the balcony, and it seemed as if there were thousands of steps leading up to a great mountain. On the steps were packages wrapped in beautiful paper—like Christmas, birthday, or anniversary wrapping paper. Some of the packages were huge and others were as small as a diamond ring. The angel on the balcony explained that these packages are the gifts that God has for humanity, but because we pray amiss, He has not been able to release them to us.

And in that vision God began to whisper to me in a language that my physical ears couldn't understand, but my spirit was able to comprehend. He explained that when we pray, we should pray for the release of what He has for us and stop settling for mediocrity.

The apostle John wrote in 3 John 2, "*Beloved, I pray that you may prosper in all things and be in health, just as your soul prospers.*" But there are satanic forces that come against our prosperity.

The more time you spend with God and get into His Word, the less time you will have to listen to your sinful nature and to the devil with his deceptions.

The "Lure Demon"

Many people do not realize that spiritual warfare is involved in overcoming certain hindrances in their lives. Recently, I was in deep prayer and intercession with some ministers I had invited to my house. We were seeking God's guidance for the upcoming year. The Spirit of the Lord fell on me, and I began to see a vision. God took me into a wooded area where there were demon powers suspended in the air. They were the worst-looking demons I'd ever seen. One of them actually looked like a ten-foot-long lure, similar to lures used to catch fish. It was snakelike, and its eyes were looking around for prey. There was another demon covered in hair. I could discern that it had seducing powers. Then, I saw other demons in the shape of monkeys. All types of demonic activities were present.

The more time you spend in God's Word, the less time you have to listen to Satan's deceptions.

As the ministers and I began to pray, I saw the Holy Spirit come in like a flood. It really was like water flowing in that came out through the valleys, the mountains, and the hills. Yet in this Spirit of the Lord there was fire, and the fire began to chase these evil presences and to cremate them. They'd burn up and turn into ashes. I had these visions all night long as I was in prayer and meditation.

Seducing demons, including the "lure demon," are in the world today. They are inciting people to lust after everything except the things of God. They are actually luring them into rebellion against the will of God. This is why believers must learn how to overcome by the blood of the Lamb and the word of their testimony. (See Revelation 12:11.)

Once we recognize the activities of these demons, we have more compassion for people who are struggling to obey the will of God. We begin to see that this demonic activity is what has hindered many souls from being saved. Many people are not born again because, unbeknownst to them, these powers have enticed them away from God. They're not even aware that they have gotten into a trap until it has almost completely overpowered them. Only through the grace of God and the blood of Jesus can they be delivered from these seducing powers. It touched my soul and tugged on my compassion when I saw the depth of the deception that these luring spirits have over people who are not connected to God.

We often hear people testify, "God, thank You for delivering me from a miserable life of sin!" Yet the misery of sin is usually in its consequences because, as we are committing it, it brings our flesh much pleasure. That is why it takes the power of God to be delivered from many of the things that we find impossible to shake. If sin were not pleasurable, the devil would not have anything with which to tempt us. He only uses what we desire, and desire is filled with things that appease our flesh. This is not to say that all desire is sin, but rather that all temptation involves pleasure, for without the desire, we cannot be tempted.

Don't drown out the "nagging" voice of your conscience when tempted to sin.

For instance, if you have a distaste for seafood, no matter how persistently the waiter offers it to you, you will continue to refuse it—even to the point of becoming disgruntled about his continued persistence. But if you are a notorious beefeater and that same waiter offers you a porterhouse steak, your glands will begin salivating even before he brings it to the table. Despite the doctor's orders against eating too much red meat, you will eat as much as your appetite can handle and settle for dealing with the consequences of your gluttonous appetite later.

That is how sin often works. We don't just fall into it, but we are drawn into it by our own desires. Even though we know it has consequences, we often drown out that "nagging" voice called the conscience in return for the opportunity to indulge in "irresistible" desires.

This is the same process that makes an addict's habit so gripping—the overwhelming desire that his appetite has developed for the addictive substance. If an addict is not delivered, he becomes a slave to his god, the object of his addiction; nothing but the true and living God will be able to draw him away from it. Above their jobs, families, relationships, finances, and successes, addicts will continue to be overpowered by the seducing spirits of their addictions.

Countless addicts leave rehabilitation centers each day having deceived family members into believing that they've conquered the debilitating grip of addiction. Not only are these destructive addictions a disease, but they also involve a spirit of deception. Many of our youth never get the opportunity to experience the joys of a positive, productive life because they have turned their lives over to the demonic deception of the experience of a drug "high."

Drug addiction is not necessarily a welcome desire for those who have succumbed to it, but it is one that will remain until they submit the god of their desires to the God of their deliverance. It isn't that many addicts want to remain in that condition, but their desire for what is controlling them will not allow them to break free without a fight.

Destructive addictions are not only a disease, but they also involve a spirit of deception.

Therefore, those who minister to people suffering from debilitating addictions must understand that the addict is being controlled by forces much more evil than the substance itself. They must pray for the addict's deliverance from the evil forces of deception and seduction. They also must pray that he or she will have the power and strength of the Lord to resist the temptation, which may remain strong long after the addict has been set free.

On the beach near my home in Florida, the locals shared with me a powerful testimony of a young man whose life had been miraculously transformed by listening to the Word of God. This young man was invited to a Bible study on the beach during a very critical time in his life. He would have his Bible open, but he would have his cocaine hidden inside it, and he'd snort the cocaine while the preacher was talking about the Lord.

He explained, "I would remember a few words: 'Jesus saves; Jesus loves you.' And I believed that Bible stuff. I would study the Bible when I was as high as a kite, and I did that for almost a month. I just wanted to be around people who were happy and loved the Lord. The preacher didn't know I was taking that cocaine, but God knew. One day I was sitting there, and I was getting ready to take more cocaine, but I had no desire for it. The desire was leaving me. And I thought, *Boy, this is strange.*"

Then the young man began to listen to the minister talk about how Jesus loved him and how He wanted to set people free from destructive habits. So he cried out to the Lord, "God, this is a habit. This is a bad habit. It's wrong, and it's destroying my life. Would You please deliver me from this habit? I'll be honest, Lord. I like it, but now I have no desire for what is going on." He said a simple prayer to God, and all at once he felt something like warm liquid come over him from the crown of his head to the soles of his feet. He felt a bubbling come out of his soul, and he began to praise the Lord. He knew God was delivering him and taking away that desire. He explained that this was the beginning of his deliverance.

"Days and weeks went by, and I kept going to that Bible study. It took the Lord a while with me. I didn't do any more cocaine, but I would drink heavily. Yet the more I sat under the Bible study, the more I would listen. The more no one condemned me, pointed a finger at me, or told me that God hated me, the more I began to know this God and to understand Him. He was there for me no matter what, and I said, 'God, make me a great overcomer; make me a minister,' and God began to do that with me. And now I am totally delivered and totally set free through the Word of the Lord and through His power."

We must pray for addicts not only to be delivered, but also to be able to resist future temptation.

Today, you may be bound in a similar way. Perhaps you have no peace or joy. Through the enemy's deception, and through other things that have gone wrong in your life, you may be out of money. Perhaps you have been put in jail because you committed crimes that you wish you had never done. You may have suffered tremendously from the destructive power of drugs, alcohol, and abusive situations. But God is just a prayer away, and even if you can't talk out loud, you can talk to Him in your heart. You don't have to make a spectacle of yourself to get God's attention. Seek to put Him first in everything. The Bible says that we are to love the Lord our God with all our mind, all our heart, all our soul, and all our strength. (See Mark 12:30.)

GROW IN GRACE

Satan works in subtle and various ways to keep people from knowing the heavenly Father or to get them to turn away from Him. Those who do not yet know the Lord must turn to God and ask Him to deliver them, just as the young man from Florida did. Christians also must watch over their lives and overcome the sinful nature through the power of the Holy Spirit. They must make sure they are not being influenced by demonic forces that want them to have impure hearts before God and to succumb to religiosity, bitterness, pride, spiritual immaturity, and various addictions. As Peter admonished,

Be diligent to be found by Him in peace, without spot and blameless; and consider that the longsuffering of our Lord is salvation....Beware lest you also fall from your own steadfastness, being led away with the error of the wicked; but grow in the grace and knowledge of our Lord and Savior Jesus Christ.

(2 Peter 3:14–15, 17–18)

Chapter 7

A Sacrificed Life

An essential aspect of walking close to God and experiencing the manifestations of answered prayers, as well as dreams and visions, is the ability to embrace aloneness. People who constantly need others around them will never be able to fully experience the type of relationship with God that those who spend quality time with Him are blessed to experience. For it is during those times of intimacy and quietness that the voice of God resounds and His mysteries are unraveled. We begin to develop a greater understanding of the necessity of His presence and power in our lives.

In the midst of stress and trials, we often attempt to find comfort and advice from family, friends, and even acquaintances. This is fine as long as you have sought God first and you never allow the voice of humankind to override God's instructions. The securest place to find rest is in the presence of God. *"In repentance and rest is your salvation, in quietness and trust is your strength"* (Isaiah 30:15 NIV). Jesus said,

> *Come to Me, all you who labor and are heavy laden, and I will give you rest. Take My yoke upon you and learn from Me, for I am gentle and lowly in heart, and you will find rest for your souls. For My yoke is easy and My burden is light.*
>
> (Matthew 11:28–30)

Resting in the Yoke of Jesus

Taking the *"yoke"* of Christ not only gives us rest, but it also helps us to develop intimacy with God. When people come in contact with you, they should be able to feel His presence by the peace that exudes from you as His child. How do you take this yoke upon yourself? Jesus gives us three instructions for entering into His rest.

"Come to Me"

Coming to Jesus means surrendering your life to Him and looking to Him in all things. Our Father loves it when we pray to Him in Jesus' name, asking for advice and direction, because it shows we acknowledge Him as the All-knowing One. Don't just go to God after all else has failed. Instead, save yourself some trouble, and go to God first!

"Take My Yoke upon You"

Jesus' yoke is not burdensome. Rather, it is the means of our receiving proper direction in life. In the physical world, a yoke is defined as "a wooden bar or frame by which two draft animals (as oxen) are joined at the heads or necks for working together."[5] When we take upon ourselves the yoke of Jesus, we are to follow His movements as He guides us. He is the One who steers us in the way that we should go. He also equips us with the foresight and the strength to graze in green pastures and continue plowing in the paths of righteousness for His name's sake. (See Psalm 23:3.) This is why Jesus said, *"For my yoke is easy and my burden is light"* (Matthew 11:30).

> *Jesus' "yoke" is the means of our receiving proper direction in life.*

The yoke seems hard only when we are trying to pull away from Christ and go in a direction He is not taking us. And the burden becomes too heavy to bear only when we begin taking on more than what God has ordained for us to carry.

> *God is faithful; he will not let you be tempted beyond what you can bear. But when you are tempted, he will also provide*

[5] *Merriam-Webster's 11th Collegiate Dictionary*, s.v., "yoke."

a way out so that you can stand up under it. (1 Corinthians 10:13 NIV)

God is not in the business of destroying us with burdens. He came to set the captives free! (See John 3:17.) If you are currently yoked with a crippling bondage and are no longer able to stand, you can know for certain that it is not ordained by God. Cast down this bondage, go to God, and get your deliverance immediately.

For the weapons of our warfare are not carnal but mighty in God for pulling down strongholds, casting down arguments and every high thing that exalts itself against the knowledge of God, bringing every thought into captivity to the obedience of Christ. (2 Corinthians 10:4–5)

"Learn of Me"

The only way to learn of Jesus is to spend time with Him and to become familiar with His voice. Learn to embrace time alone with Him as a blessing and not a burden.

Show me your ways, O Lord, teach me your paths; guide me in your truth and teach me, for you are God my Savior, and my hope is in you all day long.
(Psalm 25:4–5 NIV)

Block out all distractions and make up your mind that you will not allow anything to prevent you from discerning the Lord's voice, as opposed to that of the devil or even your own sinful nature.

> *But he who enters by the door is the shepherd of the sheep. To him the doorkeeper opens, and the sheep hear his voice; and he calls his own sheep by name and leads them out. And when he brings out his own sheep, he goes before them; and the sheep follow him, for they know his voice. Yet they will by no means follow a stranger, but will flee from him, for they do not know the voice of strangers....My sheep hear My voice, and I know them, and they follow Me.* (John 10:2–5, 27)

Throughout the Word of God, we are encouraged to prioritize our lifestyles according to God's will and not our own. We can do this as we learn of Jesus. Second Chronicles 16:9 says, *"For the eyes of the Lord run to and fro throughout the whole earth, to show Himself strong on behalf of those whose heart is loyal to Him."* Matthew 6:33 says, *"Seek first the kingdom of God and His righteousness, and all these things shall be added to you."* Proverbs 31:30 says, *"Charm is deceitful and beauty is passing, but a woman who fears the*

Lord, she shall be praised." The word *fear* does not mean to "quake in terror" but rather to revere God as the divine Ruler of all things.

> *Trust in the* Lord *with all your heart, and lean not on your own understanding; in all your ways acknowledge Him, and He shall direct your paths. Do not be wise in your own eyes; fear the* Lord *and depart from evil. It will be health to your flesh, and strength to your bones.*
>
> (Proverbs 3:5–8)

I need to caution you against trying to hear God's voice without having a good knowledge of His Word. Have you ever met up with someone who spends hours in prayer but comes out of his or her prayer closet with false doctrines or *"doctrines of demons"* (1 Timothy 4:1)? How does this happen? The devil can disguise himself as *"an angel of light"* (2 Corinthians 11:14). Keep reading the Scriptures so that when something does not line up with the Word, you will be equipped with the proper knowledge to cast it down immediately.

Alone in His Presence

When God separates you unto Himself, it's for the purpose of training and teaching you. He wants you to become familiar with His voice. He desires that His Spirit become a vital presence in your everyday life. God wants to use this time to impart His nuggets of wisdom, knowledge, and truth into your life and for you to become totally dependent upon His anointing to lead and guide you. You must get to the place where His presence is so prominent in your life that it no longer feels unusual to rely upon His Spirit—even in the midst of adversity, trials, and rejection.

Knowledge of God's Word helps ensure we are truly hearing His voice.

You may be at a point in your life where you feel lonely, that no one cares about your situation, or that God has forgotten about you. I want you to know that although it can sometimes feel like a lonely life, there are occasions when God wants to separate you to do a great work for Him in the body of Christ. It can seem lonely because it requires a lot of time and prayer. It necessitates an understanding of your commitment to God to pray and intercede at a moment's notice.

Sometimes, we can get into a frame of mind where we just want to get alone and be with God. At other times, however, we want to be out doing things, such as shopping, going to dinner, or attending a sports event. Women, especially, are made up in such a way that they need close friends for emotional support. Sometimes, a woman just needs to find her best friend so they can have a good cry together.

Deep in their hearts, most women love their children and families; they love the work that they do and the sacrifices that they make each day, and they are satisfied. Eventually, however, loneliness creeps up on them, and this can cause them to become discouraged and distracted. At those times, they have to use the Word of God to steer themselves back onto the right path.

The Word of God will ultimately bring us all through every trial and tribulation that we face. You need to trust God and know that He would not have given you such great responsibility if He did not have faith in you to carry it out through His strength.

A Vision of Sacrificed Lives

Once, while I was in deep intercession at home, I was seeking God regarding some situations in my life and God began to speak to me about a sacrificed life. I was awake, but He revealed a vision, and I could actually see the things in action that I was praying for at the time, as the Scriptures seemed to come alive. I saw some things written on a scroll. The glory of God surrounded it so that I was unable to read what was written on it. Then I saw a stairway going from earth up toward heaven. A big, beautiful cloud hovered above the stairway, and there were many glorious angels standing upon the stairs. Their fine clothing was like that of kings and queens. The angels held trays in their hands. These trays were probably about a foot and a half long and a foot wide. Upon each tray rested a transparent, round, white object. These objects looked like pieces of light fog, but each of them was extremely pure and emitted the essence of cleanliness. They were not inanimate objects; it was obvious that they exuded the essence of life. Each of them moved ever so gently across its tray but never fell off.

Get to the place where it no longer feels unusual to rely on God's Spirit.

I continued watching this vision as the angels went through the gates of heaven. Shouting and praises went up toward God. Amazingly, when I saw this vision, a lot of the loneliness that I had been experiencing suddenly left me. Even though I had been having a pity party for myself, God was gracious to me and gave me peace.

Then I saw three huge altars. The first altar looked like it was made out of bronze and gold, and the one in front of it was smaller but beautiful and glorious. It looked like it was made out of stone, covered with some type of material that glistened. The third altar was in front of God Himself, and it was a huge, high altar. The first altar read "Sacrifice Altar," the second "Mercy Seat," and the third "the Altar of God."

God was sitting on a throne, but I couldn't see His face because it was full of light and power. I could, however, see His arms, His robe, and His hands. Above the throne, a beautiful white cloud was suspended in the air, and around the throne I could smell fragrances. Approximately six feet over from the altars stood Jesus. His back was turned toward me, but I knew it was the Lord.

"Oh, my Lord!" I began to shout with excitement.

The angels, still holding the trays, were all kneeling down at the smaller altar with their heads bowed, and there stood Jesus. I saw Him lift His left hand and rest it upon His stomach. He bent to begin interceding for the sacrificed lives. He reached His right arm toward these angels and continued to travail and groan before the Father. Then, all of the angels stood behind Him in a line as the travail went on, and I heard a voice tell me to look.

I looked on the other side of the three altars, and there I saw a huge wall with doors made out of solid gold. They were small doors, about two feet by two feet, and each one had writing on it. Out of these doors came power, light, and glory.

I thought to myself, *This looks familiar to me.* All at once I realized that the small doors resembled compartments in a mausoleum, on which the names of the deceased are written. There was lettering on each door and a handle attached to it. I stared at this scene until an angel said to me, "Look! Behold what God is going to do."

We must trust God and say, "Whatever pleases You is what I want to do."

I turned and looked back at Jesus and noticed that He had stopped travailing. He got on His knees, then stood up and raised both hands. The Father motioned for an angel and said, "Lay the sacrificed life down on the Sacrifice Altar." The angel that was with me said, "That is the life of someone who has died to self. That is their sacrificed life. The angels have brought it here, and it is being laid before God upon the Sacrifice Altar. If God receives it, then He will have the angels put it over in those long drawers...behind those doors."

The angels began to move back, and I heard the voice of God, like many waters, say, "I will receive that sacrificed life." The angels shouted. Jesus praised the Father, and They talked together. A scroll was brought out before God. He wrote down some things, and they rolled it up. I heard the word *archives*.

Then, one of the larger angels, standing with a sword, opened up the top drawer. He picked up this tray with the sacrificed life upon it and put it inside the drawer, shut the door, and wrote, "Received...Approved...Accepted." He also wrote the date and time. When he shut the door, it sealed up automatically with a solid gold seal. When I saw this, I thought, *Oh, Lord, the earth doesn't really know what it means to have a "sacrificed life."* God really means for us to die to ourselves. He means we must die to our sinful natures and let God's nature and ways arise within us. I also saw written upon this door the name of the person whose sacrificial life had been accepted and the call of God that was upon his or her life.

I watched this process for hours; however, sometimes the sacrifice was rejected, and the Lord would say, "I do not receive that sacrificed life." So the angels would bow their heads, weep, and take the trays back down to the earth. I thought to myself, *This is so serious!* And I knew then that Jesus is interceding for us to die to our sinful natures and to obey God, even when loneliness is present.

It's very important for you to know that God takes notice of everything. I know sometimes we can begin feeling as if we're in a rut, but we have to continue standing on His Word, regardless of what is going on in our lives. Our souls are important to God. He does not want anybody to go to hell. After this vision, I began to seek the Lord more about my own life, and I repented for complaining.

God will give you much wisdom and knowledge, not just for your own use, but for you to use for His glory. When God has chosen you as a vessel through whom He can work, it takes sacrifice to fulfill His calling upon your life. It takes time to pray, study, and intercede, which means that you must learn how to balance out your time. Then you must learn how to trust Him enough to say, "God, whatever pleases You the most is what I want to do." God is not rigid. He doesn't want you to be like a puppet on a string. He wants you to enjoy your life and enjoy the Word of the Lord.

Keep Moving Forward in the Lord

Once, I was seeking the Lord and thanking and praising Him, and the angel of the Lord said, "I have a nugget of truth to share with the people." Suddenly, the Scripture came to me, *"Whoever will not receive you nor hear your words, when you depart from that house or city, shake off the dust from your feet"* (Matthew 10:14). In the context of the sacrificed life, I interpret this verse to mean that when people do you wrong and things happen that you don't understand, you should continue to keep your focus and not allow those things to keep you from moving forward in the things of God.

I saw a vision of someone shaking the dust off his feet, and there were angels underneath the feet actually catching the dust in containers. As I watched them catch the dust, they closed the lids, labeled them, and took them to heaven. In heaven there was a huge table with many holy men sitting around it, and they put these containers on the table. When the dust from the feet came out of those containers and landed on the table, it created written words. The words made from the dust spelled out the transgressions that had been committed, which had prompted the dust to be shaken from the feet.

The holy men began to read these particles of dust and to write out the words on paper. Then, these writings were all labeled and put into the books of those who had done these things. They took all these records to a record room where other men looked them over. This room looked similar to a courtroom. Jesus was there at a table giving orders, and as He reviewed each book, He would write something on different scrolls and different papers and give them to the angels. He would also command them to come to the earth and answer our prayers. So you see, everything that the Bible says is very important. We have a God who cares about everything we do, and He cares about every wrong thing that is done to us, too.

> *Turn to the Lord and yield yourself to Him as a sacrificed life.*

It's time to pray and to seek the counsel of the Lord. We must turn to the Lord with pure hearts and yield ourselves to Him as sacrificed lives.

> *I beseech you therefore, brethren, by the mercies of God, that you present your bodies a living sacrifice, holy, acceptable to God, which is your reasonable service.*
> (Romans 12:1)

Chapter 8

Attitudes and Qualities of Intercessors

God has been bringing back to my remembrance many of the things that He showed me originally when I wrote the book *A Divine Revelation of Hell*. He has been revealing to me that we are in a time of the greatest move of God, but it is also a time when many people in our society have lost reverence for God. There are all kinds of perversions, widespread hatred, and frequent murders. Even many ministers are developing a mind-set of "anything goes."

> *The people of the land have used oppressions, committed robbery, and mistreated the poor and needy; and they wrongfully oppress the stranger. So I sought for a man among them who would make a wall, and stand in the gap before Me on behalf of the land, that I should not destroy it; but I found no one.* (Ezekiel 22:29–30)

Today, we are in great need of real intercessors—those who will "stand in the gap" and pray for our country and our world. Prayer has the power to set the captives free because it connects the intercessor to the All-powerful One. When you encounter a person who is accustomed to speaking to God and hearing from Him, you find an individual ready to roll up his or her spiritual sleeves of prayer and fight the good fight of faith without hesitation.

Let us look at some of the attitudes and qualities that are essential in believers who want to be effective in intercession.

Alignment with Jesus and the Holy Spirit

First, as intercessors, we must understand that Jesus and the Holy Spirit are interceding for us, and that when we intercede, we need to be aligned with God's will.

Jesus Is Interceding

> [Jesus], *because He continues forever, has an unchangeable priesthood. Therefore He is also able to save to the uttermost those who come to God through Him, since He always lives to make intercession for them. For such a High Priest was fitting for us,*

> *who is holy, harmless, undefiled, separate from sinners, and has become higher than the heavens.* (Hebrews 7:24–26)

The book of Hebrews tells us that Jesus, as our High Priest, is right now *"seated at the right hand of the throne of the Majesty in the heavens"* (Hebrews 8:1). He sacrificed Himself on our behalf, and now that He has returned to the Father, He is interceding for our spiritual preservation. Let us read carefully this revealing passage from John 17, where Jesus prayed to the Father just before His crucifixion:

> *I do not pray for the world but for those whom You have given Me, for they are Yours. And all Mine are Yours, and Yours are Mine, and I am glorified in them. Now I am no longer in the world, but these are in the world, and I come to You. Holy Father, keep through Your name those whom You have given Me, that they may be one as We are. While I was with them in the world, I kept them in Your name. Those whom You gave Me I have kept; and none of them is lost except the son of perdition, that the Scripture might be fulfilled. But now I come to You, and these things I speak in the world, that they may have My joy fulfilled in themselves. I have given them*

Your word; and the world has hated them because they are not of the world, just as I am not of the world. I do not pray that You should take them out of the world, but that You should keep them from the evil one. They are not of the world, just as I am not of the world. Sanctify them by Your truth. Your word is truth. As You sent Me into the world, I also have sent them into the world. And for their sakes I sanctify Myself, that they also may be sanctified by the truth. I do not pray for these alone, but also for those who will believe in Me through their word; that they all may be one, as You, Father, are in Me, and I in You; that they also may be one in Us, that the world may believe that You sent Me. And the glory which You gave Me I have given them, that they may be one just as We are one: I in them, and You in Me; that they may be made perfect in one, and that the world may know that You have sent Me, and have loved them as You have loved Me. Father, I desire that they also whom You gave Me may be with Me where I am, that they may behold My glory which You have given Me; for You loved Me before the foundation of the world. (John 17:9–24)

Jesus prayed (1) that believers would live in unity, just as He is one with the Father, (2) that we would have the same joy He has, (3) that we would be kept from the evil one, (4) that we would be sanctified by God's truth, (5) that we would have unity with other believers and with the Father and the Son, (6) that we would be witnesses to the world of the truth of the gospel because of this unity, and (7) that one day we would live with Jesus and see His glory.

When we are at a loss for words, the Spirit intercedes on our behalf.

As we pray, we can intercede along the same lines for ourselves and others. Jesus said that we can pray to the Father in His name, and that our requests will be answered:

> *If two of you agree on earth concerning anything that they ask, it will be done for them by My Father in heaven. For where two or three are gathered together in My name, I am there in the midst of them.*
> (Matthew 18:19–20)

> *He who believes in Me, the works that I do he will do also; and greater works than these he will do, because I go to My Father.*

> *And whatever you ask in My name, that I will do, that the Father may be glorified in the Son. If you ask anything in My name, I will do it.* (John 14:12–14)

> *You did not choose Me, but I chose you and appointed you that you should go and bear fruit, and that your fruit should remain, that whatever you ask the Father in My name He may give you.* (John 15:16)

The Holy Spirit Is Interceding

The Bible also assures us that God's Holy Spirit intercedes for us:

> *The Spirit also helps in our weaknesses. For we do not know what we should pray for as we ought, but the Spirit Himself makes intercession for us with groanings which cannot be uttered. Now He who searches the hearts knows what the mind of the Spirit is, because He makes intercession for the saints according to the will of God.* (Romans 8:26–27)

When we are at a loss for words, the Holy Spirit steps in to intercede on our behalf. He communicates what we would pray if we only had the understanding and the words to say it. We should never view prayer as a laborious task because the Spirit is there to help us.

We Are to Intercede

Knowing that Jesus and the Holy Spirit are interceding for our spiritual strength and success, we are to become intercessors, as well, praying for God's kingdom to come and His will to be done on earth as it is in heaven. (See Matthew 6:10.) Ask God to baptize you with His Holy Spirit so that you may pray to God through a Spirit-given prayer language in the *"tongues of men and of angels"* (1 Corinthians 13:1) as you address the many needs in your life and others' lives. (See, for example, Mark 16:17; Acts 2:1–11; 1 Corinthians 12:5–11; 14:39.)

Intercede for God's kingdom to come and His will to be done on earth as it is in heaven.

The apostle Paul wrote, *"I will pray with the spirit, and I will also pray with the understanding. I will sing with the spirit, and I will also sing with the understanding"* (1 Corinthians 14:15). We are to pray according to the will of God and ask that the Holy Spirit would speak through us to say the right words. Then we are to yield ourselves to

God and allow His Spirit to pray through us as we trust and believe Him.

> *Beloved, building yourselves up on your most holy faith, praying in the Holy Spirit, keep yourselves in the love of God.*
>
> (Jude 20–21)

> *Praying always with all prayer and supplication in the Spirit, being watchful to this end with all perseverance and supplication for all the saints.*
>
> (Ephesians 6:18)

WILLINGNESS AND FAITHFULNESS

Effective intercessors have a willingness to intercede on behalf of God's work in the world and are faithful in doing so. They are available and ready to pray, as these Scriptures encourage:

> *Continuing steadfastly in prayer.*
>
> (Romans 12:12)

> *Do not be anxious about anything, but in everything, by prayer and petition, with thanksgiving, present your requests to God.* (Philippians 4:6 NIV)

> *Devote yourselves to prayer, being watchful and thankful.* (Colossians 4:2 NIV)

Pray without ceasing.
(1 Thessalonians 5:17)

I want men everywhere to lift up holy hands in prayer, without anger or disputing. (1 Timothy 2:8 NIV)

Once when I was living in Michigan, I was in deep intercession when a vision came before me of a car turned upside down with somebody pinned in it. I could not see who it was, but I knew I was praying for that individual. I prayed almost six hours that day, and after I was done, I went about my daily chores. Throughout the rest of the day, however, I thought about that prayer.

Sometime later, I was visiting some of my relatives, and we were talking about visions and prayer. I shared with them the vision of the car that I had seen during prayer, and one of my relatives responded, "That was me! My car was a convertible and turned over in the mud. I was pinned inside that car, and I could not breathe. I was dying, but then all at once I felt something lift the car up off of my body, and I was able to crawl out through the mud up to the road!"

"Thank You, Lord, that You saw fit to use me to pray!" I said. And everyone around me knew an angel of the Lord had lifted that car off my loved one during that critical moment. Miraculously, despite such a horrendous accident, my relative had been released from the hospital with no significant injury.

You can see why it is so very important to be faithful in prayer, especially when God is showing you a vision. Even when you do not feel like it, you should cry out to the Lord because someone's life could be depending upon your obedience.

Reverence for God and Righteousness

We talked in earlier chapters about our need for a pure heart, but since righteousness is so essential for effective prayer, it is important to mention it here, as well. *"The effective, fervent prayer of a righteous man avails much"* (James 5:16). True intercessors who pray for God's will to come on earth reverence His name, and they are in right relationship with Him.

> *Teach me Your way, O Lord; I will walk in Your truth; unite my heart to fear Your name. I will praise You, O Lord my God, with all my heart, and I will glorify Your name forevermore.* (Psalm 86:11–12)

> *For you are the temple of the living God. As God has said: "I will dwell in them and*

> *walk among them. I will be their God, and they shall be My people." Therefore "come out from among them and be separate, says the Lord. Do not touch what is unclean, and I will receive you. I will be a Father to you, and you shall be My sons and daughters, says the* Lord *Almighty." Therefore, having these promises, beloved, let us cleanse ourselves from all filthiness of the flesh and spirit, perfecting holiness in the fear of God.* (2 Corinthians 6:16–7:1)

> *For the eyes of the* Lord *are on the righteous, and His ears are open to their prayers; but the face of the* Lord *is against those who do evil.* (1 Peter 3:12)

Knowledge of Who God Is, and Knowledge of Who You Are in God

Effective intercessors also recognize the significance of knowing who God is and who they are in God through Christ Jesus. In 1 Kings 18:20–40, we read about a standoff between Elijah and the prophets of Baal on Mount Carmel regarding who was the true God. The people of Israel were involved in worshipping this false god. They apparently wanted to be the people of the living God in name only while worshipping an idol. Elijah asked them,

"How long will you falter between two opinions? If the Lord is God, follow Him; but if Baal, follow him." But the people answered him not a word. (1 Kings 18: 21)

Once you know who your God is, you will not allow yourself to become engaged in heated arguments with people who have no intention of changing their opinions. Instead, you allow the life of Christ shining through you to reveal the truth of the gospel. Similarly, Elijah let God's power speak for Him. In a bold step, he issued a challenge. He and the prophets of Baal would both offer sacrifices on separate altars. Whichever sacrifice was consumed by heavenly fire was the one belonging to the true and living God.

Allow Christ's life to shine through you and reveal the truth of the gospel.

Elijah let Baal's prophets go first. They exhausted themselves, crying out to Baal with no results. Then, as if this weren't enough, Elijah went so far as to douse his sacrifice and the entire trench around the altar with water, as an extra handicap in the contest. Yet not even the water prevented Elijah's sacrifice from being consumed by the Lord God's fire:

> *Then the fire of the* LORD *fell and consumed the burnt sacrifice, and the wood and the stones and the dust, and it licked up the water that was in the trench. Now when all the people saw it, they fell on their faces; and they said, "The* LORD, *He is God! The* LORD, *He is God!"*
>
> (1 Kings 18:38–39)

Do you know the power and greatness of God? Do you know who you are as a child of God through Christ Jesus? Paul wrote, *"You are complete in* [Christ], *who is the head of all principality and power"* (Colossians 2:10), and *"Be strong in the Lord and in the power of His might"* (Ephesians 6:10). Intercessors win battles with the mighty Word of God and by the strength of His Spirit.

> *For the weapons of our warfare are not carnal but mighty in God for pulling down strongholds, casting down arguments and every high thing that exalts itself against the knowledge of God, bringing every thought into captivity to the obedience of Christ.* (2 Corinthians 10:4)

> *"Not by might nor by power, but by My Spirit," says the* LORD *of hosts.*
>
> (Zechariah 4:6)

The intercessor's rationale is, "If God said it, then what's the problem?" This was exactly David's attitude when He encountered Goliath intimidating the Israelite army. He inquired of the men, *"For who is this uncircumcised Philistine, that he should defy the armies of the* ***living God****?"* (1 Samuel 17:26, emphasis added).

First, David knew He was serving the all-powerful and living God, just as Ezekiel had. As the Scripture says,

> *O LORD God of Israel, the One who dwells between the cherubim, You are God, You alone, of all the kingdoms of the earth. You have made heaven and earth.*
>
> (2 Kings 19:15)

Second, David knew that God fights on behalf of His people.

> *The eternal God is your refuge, and underneath are the everlasting arms; He will thrust out the enemy from before you, and will say, "Destroy!"*
>
> (Deuteronomy 33:27)

David felt insulted that a Philistine would have the nerve to stand against the children of God. In other words, "How dare someone who doesn't honor our God come against His people!"

The problem, however, was that His people were unsure of their identity in Him, as well as the power that they possessed in Him. The same unfortunate fact holds true for many of God's people today. If you remain unsure of your power through Christ Jesus, you will continue to bow down to the Goliaths in your life instead of defeating them. Prayer is our weapon against the devices of Satan. As boldly as David confronted and overcame Goliath, we must be equally brazen in resisting the demonic forces that dare to challenge those who belong to God. Personalize David's decree and make it your own. No matter what tactic Satan uses to try to take away your peace of mind or to harm others, stare him in the face and declare,

If you remain unsure of your power through Christ Jesus, you will continue to bow down to the Goliaths in your life.

> *You come to me with a sword, with a spear, and with a javelin* [substitute whatever weapon the enemy is trying to use to destroy you]. *But I come to you in the name of the* Lord *of hosts, the God of the armies*

> *of Israel....This day the* LORD *will deliver you into my hand, and I will strike you and take your head from you.*
> (1 Samuel 17:45–46)

FAITH

Another essential quality for prayer is having faith, which comes from learning who God is through His Word. *"So then faith comes by hearing, and hearing by the word of God"* (Romans 10:17). Many times, when we are attempting to defeat the enemy, we think the solution is found in some deep spiritual mystery, or we seek power in others instead of going to God in prayer for ourselves. Faith is the one component that sets apart those who have great power in prayer from those who continually seek others to pray for them.

Believers rely not on earthly sight but on the perfect vision of God.

"Where there is no vision, the people perish: but he that keepeth the law, happy is he" (Proverbs 29:18 KJV). As believers, we rely not on our earthly sight but upon the perfect vision of God. *"Now faith is the substance of things hoped for, the evidence of things not seen"* (Hebrews 11:1). We

cannot always trust our physical eyes and ears to reveal the will of God; we must be able to connect with Him spiritually and learn of Him through His Word.

Faith-filled prayer brings powerful results:

> *Elijah was a man with a nature like ours, and he prayed earnestly that it would not rain; and it did not rain on the land for three years and six months. And he prayed again, and the heaven gave rain, and the earth produced its fruit.* (James 5:17–18)

> *Assuredly, I say to you, if you have faith and do not doubt, you will not only do what was done to the fig tree, but also if you say to this mountain, "Be removed and be cast into the sea," it will be done. And whatever things you ask in prayer, believing, you will receive.*
> (Matthew 21:21–22)

Compassion

The quality of compassion is also necessary for effective prayer. Motivated by compassion, Jesus taught the spiritually hungry, fed the physically hungry, healed the sick, and delivered the oppressed. For example, the Scriptures record the following:

> *When He saw the multitudes,* ***He was moved with compassion for them****, because they were weary and scattered, like sheep having no shepherd. Then He said to His disciples, "The harvest truly is plentiful, but the laborers are few. Therefore pray the Lord of the harvest to send out laborers into His harvest."*
>
> (Matthew 9:36–38, emphasis added)

> *And when Jesus went out He saw a great multitude; and* ***He was moved with compassion for them****, and healed their sick.* (Matthew 14:14, emphasis added)

> *Two blind men sitting by the road, when they heard that Jesus was passing by, cried out, saying, "Have mercy on us, O Lord, Son of David!" Then the multitude warned them that they should be quiet; but they cried out all the more, saying, "Have mercy on us, O Lord, Son of David!" So Jesus stood still and called them, and said, "What do you want Me to do for you?" They said to Him, "Lord, that our eyes may be opened." So* ***Jesus had compassion*** *and touched their eyes. And immediately their eyes received sight, and they followed Him.*
>
> (Matthew 20:30–34, emphasis added)

> *When He got into the boat, he who had been demon-possessed begged Him that he might be with Him. However, Jesus did not permit him, but said to him, "Go home to your friends, and tell them what great things the Lord has done for you, and* ***how He has had compassion on you****."*
>
> (Mark 5:18–19, emphasis added)

> *And when He came near the gate of the city, behold, a dead man was being carried out, the only son of his mother; and she was a widow. And a large crowd from the city was with her.* ***When the Lord saw her, He had compassion on her*** *and said to her, "Do not weep." Then He came and touched the open coffin, and those who carried him stood still. And He said, "Young man, I say to you, arise." So he who was dead sat up and began to speak. And He presented him to his mother.*
>
> (Luke 7:12–15, emphasis added)

J. Rodman Williams, Professor of Theology Emeritus at Regent University, said, "Compassion is the wellspring of miracles."[6] We are to follow Jesus' example and pray for others with

[6] J. Rodman Williams, *Great Themes of the Book II*, audio portion, Living by the Book Series, CBN (Christian Broadcasting Network).

compassion, just as Jesus reflected the compassion of the heavenly Father:

> *You, O Lord, are a God full of compassion, and gracious, longsuffering and abundant in mercy and truth.* (Psalm 86:15)

Persistence and Perseverance

True intercessors are persistent and persevering. Although you may sometimes stumble and even fall in your walk of faith, do not turn from God or give up. Regardless of what you are going through, God has an answer for every affliction. Reach out to God, and He will make you an overcomer, able to rise above everything that is trying to take you under.

Reach out to God, and He will make you an overcomer.

The Bible is filled with accounts of great men and women who overcame seemingly insurmountable obstacles due to their persistence and the power of prayer. In Genesis 18, we read that God was about to destroy Sodom because of the people's extreme wickedness. People apparently had been crying out to the Lord about injuries and injustices they had suffered at the hands of the people of this city. (See verses 20–21.)

When Abraham heard about God's plan to destroy the city, he pleaded with God for the righteous people of Sodom.

> *Would You also destroy the righteous with the wicked? Suppose there were fifty righteous within the city; would You also destroy the place and not spare it for the fifty righteous that were in it?* (Psalm 86:23–24)

Abraham continued to ask whether God would destroy the city if there were any righteous people in it, reducing the number from fifty to forty-five, then forty, thirty, twenty, and finally ten. Each time, God said He would not destroy the city if that number of righteous people were living in it.

Abraham knew that God was compassionate and would not destroy the city with undue cause. In the end, it turned out that fewer than ten righteous people lived in the city. Yet God still spared the lives of Abraham's nephew Lot and his immediate family members in response to Abraham's pleas, because He had a close relationship with Abraham. (See Genesis 18:17–19.)

> *It came to pass, when God destroyed the cities of the plain, that God remembered Abraham, and sent Lot out of the midst of the overthrow, when He overthrew the cities in which Lot had dwelt.* (Genesis 19:29)

Other people need us to persevere in prayer for them. Paul wrote to the Colossians about his fellow worker, Epaphras, *"who is one of you and a servant of Christ Jesus....He is always wrestling in prayer for you, that you may stand firm in all the will of God, mature and fully assured"* (Colossians 4:12 NIV). Epaphras "wrestled" in prayer for the Colossians so that they would be spiritually mature, confident of their standing in God, and fully obedient to Him.

One of the greatest illustrations of persistence in prayer is Jesus' parable of the widow in Luke 18:

> *Then He spoke a parable to them, that men always ought to pray and not lose heart, saying: "There was in a certain city a judge who did not fear God nor regard man. Now there was a widow in that city; and she came to him, saying, 'Get justice for me from my adversary.' And he would not for a while; but afterward he said within himself, 'Though I do not fear God nor regard man, yet because this widow troubles me I will avenge her, lest by her continual coming she weary me.'" Then the Lord said, "Hear what the unjust judge said. And shall God not avenge His own elect who cry out day and night*

to Him, though He bears long with them? I tell you that He will avenge them speedily. Nevertheless, when the Son of Man comes, will He really find faith on the earth?"

(Luke 18:1–8)

Luke wrote that Jesus gave this parable to emphasize that *"men always ought to pray and not lose heart"* (Luke 18:1). He then pointed out the widow's reward for being persistent. Even though she was pleading her case for justice before an "unjust judge," she received an answer to her request simply because she refused to give up. Many are missing out on the blessings of God because they do not sit still long enough to listen to God for an answer. Jesus was saying, in effect, "Surely, if the widow could get an answer from an unjust judge, how much more will our righteous Judge and loving heavenly Father answer our requests as we seek Him?"

People miss out because they won't sit still and listen for God's answer.

One time, my family was in the midst of selling a piece of land and we really needed the money. But every time we tried to close the transaction, the devil fought us through hindrances, through people getting sick, through the money not being there, and so forth. The devil was fighting to keep us from being prosperous. So we had to learn to keep going forward and not to give up.

You can't give up but must keep pressing on. You have to be like a hammer, hitting the devil in the head, spiritually speaking. He doesn't hear very well, so you have to continually speak God's Word against him.

When we remain persistent in our pursuit of God and in defeating the devil, then all things are possible for us through Christ Jesus. It is out of this persistence that we become prosperous and victorious. Not only can we have financial prosperity, but we also can have spiritual prosperity. God is not going to let the devil just pounce on us.

The attitudes of our hearts and the character qualities we develop through faith and obedience to God are integral parts of answered prayer. We should seek to cultivate these areas and put them into practice as we become the intercessors God desires us to be.

Chapter 9

Visions of Deliverance and Answered Prayers

The visions God gave me years ago still remain very vivid in my mind. The Lord would visit me every night and reveal shocking revelations to me as I slept. As I have described in earlier books, I was translated with Jesus to hell for three hours each night for thirty nights, and I walked among the dead. Then I went to heaven with Jesus for three hours a night for ten nights. One of the things Jesus revealed to me was how the devil orders demons to come to earth to destroy our families. For instance, if you had a relative who was just recently growing in God and about to come out of his sins, the demon would trip him up, cause him to lose money, cause accidents, and wreak all kinds of havoc in his life. Satan's demons will do everything possible to stop your loved ones from coming to God while you are praying for them.

God wants us to know that regardless of what the circumstances look like, we can't give up. We can't give up praying for ourselves, and we can't give up interceding for our loved ones. We must pray without ceasing until they come into the full knowledge of God's marvelous light and are saved and delivered.

Regardless of what people are going through or how they are behaving, you should never ask God to send judgment upon them. Your heart must be toward the Lord; it must be pure. You pray for compassion, and you pray for God to lead them. You ask God to shine His light in the darkness and destroy the works of Satan's demonic kingdom. You never curse the individuals, but you pray against the demonic spirit that's controlling them. You take dominion over the spiritual powers of darkness that are tormenting them. God wants us to pray so that salvation, revival, deliverance, and healing can take place across the nation and around the world.

God's Angels Fight for Us

In visions, I have seen chariots charge out of heaven, guided by angels who come to our rescue when we earnestly seek God in prayer. These fierce-looking war angels are focused on their purpose of fulfilling the will of God, and they fight ferociously with demons on our behalf. They have jaws of iron and eyes of fire. Their garments for warfare are made out of what looks like metal, iron, and another unidentifiable material. These angels of the Lord go all over the earth. With their huge swords of fire, they cut the evil presence and powers of darkness.

Demonic Forces Fight against Angels

Earlier, we discussed how the angel who brought the message from God to Daniel said he had been held up by opposing demonic forces. Demons will sometimes engage angels in conflict to prevent them from bringing messages from God to His people. This is why perseverance in intercession is so important.

Many of the battles we are engaged in are not physical but spiritual.

God will sometimes shake you in the middle of the night to pray. At first you may not have any idea what you're praying for, but you're actually praying that the gateways will open up to allow free passage from heaven to earth so that you and those for whom you're interceding can receive breakthroughs and deliverance. We must remember that when we pray, God hears and answers.

Yet there is a conflict in the spiritual realm between the powers of God and the powers of Satan, and it may take time for the manifestation of the answer. We are not to give up.

As I wrote about in *A Divine Revelation of Deliverance*, several times while praying, I saw visions of what looked like huge honeycombs in the sky. Angels were in bondage in these honeycombs, put there by demonic forces. I asked my intercessors to pray with me about this recurring vision. One of the intercessors saw the same vision, but he also saw another angel of the Lord with a huge sword. This angel was standing beside these honeycombs, and he said, "Ask the Lord to send help from the sanctuary."

We went into deep travail. We prayed for five hours, and as we prayed, we saw heaven open, and angels went in and ripped up those honeycombs! They carried away every one of those angels who had been in bondage and laid him in a certain area to be restored. And God began to shout, saying, "Finally someone has believed that in My Son's name, Jesus, you have dominion over the prince of the power of the air, the rulers of demon darkness, and spiritual wickedness in high places." (See Ephesians 2:2; 6:12 KJV.) When I went to heaven, I saw the deliverance army. The earth needs to know that this army is in heaven and that God uses it to wage war against the kingdom of darkness.

In Revelation 12, we see that the devil's attempts to overthrow the kingdom of God were met with defeat.

> *And war broke out in heaven: Michael and his angels fought with the dragon; and the dragon and his angels fought, but they did not prevail, nor was a place found for them in heaven any longer.*
>
> (Revelation 12:7–8)

God will not allow His kingdom or His divine plan to become corrupted by the evil tactics of the devil. That is why He helps us to uplift each other in the body of Christ through prayer and encouragement. He knows that the battles we are engaged in are not physical, as we often think, but spiritual.

Interceding for Salvation

One of our main roles in intercession is to pray for the salvation of others and to engage in spiritual warfare on their behalf. As I wrote earlier, when God prepares to show you His visions, you have to have a pure heart, and you have to be ready to listen to what He will tell you and reveal to you. This is because, after He shows you certain things, you are never the same again. You never feel the same, and you never act the same. Since the Lord appeared to me and showed me hell, I now have a burden for the lost that I had never experienced before going on my journeys with Him.

Jesus showed me that the majority of the people in hell are those who had been called by God but kept rejecting the gospel. They kept saying, "Well, tomorrow I'll get saved," until finally it was too late. The devil tricked them and then killed them. They were into idolatry, serving other gods, and putting everything else before God. In every compartment of hell, there were those who had stayed continually in their sins; there was hatred and unforgiveness. They rejected God and submitted to the works of their flesh rather than obeying God.

While we are here on earth, we have an opportunity to turn from the deceptive enticements of the devil and be saved through the washing of the blood of Jesus. We can be redeemed with *"the precious blood of Christ, as of a lamb without blemish and without spot"* (1 Peter 1:19). God loves us, and His desire is for our salvation. *"If we confess our sins, He is faithful and just to forgive us our sins and to cleanse us from all unrighteousness"* (1 John 1:9). There is healing power in the blood of Jesus. When people begin to seek God and walk in obedience to His Word, they are cleansed by the blood of the Lamb: *"If we walk in the light as He is in the light, we have fellowship with one another, and the blood of Jesus Christ His Son cleanses us from all sin"* (1 John 1:7).

In Hebrews 9, we are reminded that if the sprinkling of animal's blood was used as a ceremonial cleansing for the outward man, how much more powerful is the blood of Jesus Christ in cleansing us inside and out. (See Hebrews 9:12–14.) For Jesus entered the Most Holy Place with His own precious blood and not through the blood of an animal. (See verse 12.)

God wants people to be set free and to fulfill His will for their lives.

Once we have been redeemed by the blood of the Lamb, it is our responsibility to reveal to others how they, too, may attain the cleansing power of the blood of Christ: *"He who turns a sinner from the error of his way will save a soul from death and cover a multitude of sins"* (James 5:20). Thus, not only do we have to pray for ourselves, but we also must have a burden for those who do not know Jesus as Lord and Savior. He died so that we would have the right to eternal life.

> *Therefore I exhort first of all that supplications, prayers, intercessions, and giving of thanks be made for all men, for kings and all who are in authority, that we may lead a quiet and peaceable life in all godliness and reverence. For this is good and acceptable in the sight of God our Savior,* ***who desires all men to be saved*** *and to come to the knowledge of the truth.*
>
> (1 Timothy 2:1–4, emphasis added)

> *The Lord is not slack concerning His promise, as some count slackness, but is longsuffering toward us,* ***not willing that any should perish*** *but that all should come to repentance.*
>
> (2 Peter 3:9, emphasis added)

Regardless of what you or your loved ones are dealing with, you have to believe God's promise to wash you clean of your sins as you repent and turn to Him for salvation and help.

I have been asked the question, "If individuals love God and pray to Him, but find themselves struggling with homosexuality and lesbianism, do they go to hell?" I don't have an answer for this question, but I do know that God is a God of grace, and that His grace is there to help them. People all over the earth are suffering as they try to break free from evil spirits of homosexuality and lesbianism. These spirits can't enter just anyone. They go to people whose minds and hearts are sold out to engage in those types of acts. When you pray for people who are struggling in this way, therefore, ask the Father to release them from their bondage and their desire to sin, and instead to give them the desire to do His will.

> *If you live according to the flesh you will die; but if by the Spirit you put to death the deeds of the body, you will live. For as many as are led by the Spirit of God, these are sons of God.* (Romans 8:13–14)

Breaking Satan's Bondage

Men Entangled in Issues and Hindrances

God wants people to be set free and to be able to fulfill His will for their lives. For several years now, I've been having visions in prayer of God raising up men and women for His glory. I want to focus on what He has shown me about the men. It appeared to me as if the men were entangled with all kinds of issues. Galatians 5:1 came to me: *"Do not be entangled again with a yoke of bondage."* It seemed as if they had yokes of bondage around them and all types of hindrances. The roads before them were full of obstacles, such as money troubles, problems in their homes, and difficulties on their jobs. Those who were married faced many issues they could not resolve; but, every so often, I would see a few of them raising their hands, praising God, and being set free. The bands would just fall from them.

This vision repeated on and off for a little more than five years. As I traveled and talked to people, I learned that God had called a number of men who had never fulfilled their spiritual callings. Because of this, there was an empty place in their hearts. They knew and understood their callings, but it seemed that there was nothing they could do about them because Satan had thrown so many roadblocks and hindrances in their paths. For some of them, their marriages had ended in divorce. They could never get along with their spouses, and there were so many arguments and so much strife going on in their homes that they could not get anything done.

I began to have a heart for these men—that God would bring them out of captivity, that they would obey God, that the families would be blessed, and that the Lord would bring healing to every issue in their lives. It seemed to me that so many little children were involved and hurt in these relationships that had not been ordained by God.

I was raised in a good church, and I was taught as a child how to cast out demons. I was blessed to understand many words of the Lord, but it still didn't stop me from marrying the wrong person. My first marriage was to the wrong person because I failed to listen to the voice of God. I was young, I was foolish, and I just wanted to get away from home.

The danger of getting ahead of God is being closed to receiving His instructions.

In my heart, I knew I should have waited on the voice of the Lord, but because I didn't listen, the marriage ended in divorce five years later. I wound up causing myself a lot of heartache and grief, which easily could have been avoided if I had simply relied on the leading of the Lord. Sometimes, we get ahead of God so much that we are no longer open to receiving His instructions.

When we are born, the enemy knows when we are chosen of the Lord to fulfill a certain calling. Therefore, he sends all kinds of garbage into our lives to hinder us and even to stop us completely. He sends false romances and other seducing powers. It's like the lure demon I talked about earlier. The devil sends these seducing powers to lure us into his demonic kingdom and to stop us from doing the will of the Father.

This is why it's so important to wait on God and listen to Him for divine instructions. Even when we're young, wild, and foolish, and we think that God doesn't really talk to us, He does, and He will, if we will only learn to listen.

I sought the counsel of the Lord about what could be done for these men who were so deeply entangled in bondage. His call was very strong on many of them, but they didn't know how to break free from their bondages. I prayed that they would get involved in good churches that taught the Word of God, and I prayed for their family relationships to be healed. Every so often, I would see a vision in which some of the men were being broken free. I'd call a friend who is an intercessor, and we would pray for God to help them and their families, and for God's blessings.

As time went on, I'd see the same men in visions. Years would go by and they never could accomplish the call of God. Then I began to understand how the devil works. He wants to keep things from happening in our lives and to hinder us from understanding the call of God upon us. The devil wants us to make impromptu decisions based on emotions rather than on the divine will of God.

God's Men Marching from the Wilderness

Later, I had visions of men who were in a wooded area, standing in dry, brown leaves and twigs. They were looking up, but their eyes were closed. They seemed to be isolated from one another in this wooded area. I could see an aerial view of them, and I noticed that they were similar to the men whom I had been seeing on and off in the visions for more than five years. I could see that some were old men and others were young; they were all ages. In fact, one man looked like he was in his eighties, and I thought, *Dear God, they've struggled so long and so hard. They just can't seem to get out of this wooded area and these bondages.* It tore at my soul.

I prayed and then called a friend who is an intercessor and shared the vision with her. She immediately said, "Let's pray." We prayed for God to bring these men out, to set them free, and to heal them, because there were so many deep wounds in their hearts. I perceived in the Spirit that some of them were alone now with hardly any money. Some had lots of money but no family, and it was so sad.

Then I saw drops falling on them; the drops were blue with white light in them. Several drops would fall on the men's faces and wash around their eyes. I began to weep and cry out, "Jesus, please set these men free and let them come forth as a mighty army in the land!" As I looked at the washing of their eyes, their eyes suddenly popped open. My prayer partner asked, "Do you know what I see?"

"No," I said. "Tell me what you see, and then I'll tell you what I see."

"I see God crying and teardrops falling on these men's faces," she began to explain.

"I saw the teardrops come on their eyes and begin to wash them—huge teardrops! I thought it was a strange-looking kind of rain."

If people would truly repent, God would save them to the uttermost.

She continued, "The Lord is weeping for His men and to bring them forth so that He can use them, no matter what circumstances they've been in, and no matter what they've been through. If they would come and truly repent, God would spare them and save them to the uttermost."

Then I saw the twigs, the branches, and the entanglement fall away. There the men stood in this shadowed area, still isolated, their right legs raised, ready to march forward out of this darkness and into the light. I told my friend what I was seeing, and she had seen the same thing; so we began to seek God again for His counsel on how to pray, because we really wanted to pray exactly according to the Holy Spirit's will. We prayed and sought the counsel of the Lord, asking that the love of God would fall upon them.

As we were praying and interceding, the Spirit of the Lord brought this prophecy:

> I will speak to these dead bones, and they shall live. I shall speak to this army of men, and they shall arise. They shall come out of their caves, their mountains, their wildernesses, and I shall use them in these latter days to do a work that will amaze you; for I am the Lord your God and I shall speak, and My tears are washing over them now. And they shall march a mighty army in the land. And they shall proclaim My destiny and My Word. For these are men whom I am raising up through all their hardships. They've kept their eyes on Me. They've tried their best to do My will. But now I have sent My angels to destroy the hindrances that are around them: the briars, the thorns, the dried twigs. And I shall bring them out of this wilderness, and they shall proclaim

My Word. They shall march through the land and they shall take it. They shall take it for the Lord's sake. And the Lord is well pleased, for His righteousness' sake. For through the blood of My Son that was shed to set the captives free, this will be a delight to the Lord.

I listened to the Lord as He prophesied about His men, and I began to see a vision of the men moving forward, marching and marching straight ahead. They were not looking to the left or to the right, but they were looking straight ahead. I began to see good things being accomplished.

"I shall use them in these latter days to do a work that will amaze you."

Later on in the vision, I could see some of the men in offices, some on television, and many of them on their knees praying. Then I could see them in different aspects of the world carrying out their callings. Some were preachers and some were not, but they were all giving money for the kingdom of God to be built. I was so overjoyed to see how the hand of God had worked a great healing in their hearts and brought them forth. He truly had spoken life into those dead bones. Praise the name of the Lord!

I believe that this is the day and the hour in which God is raising up men all over the world who are business-minded and have an anointing for business and ministry. They've always had it, but now it's going to be birthed.

I also believe that God is going to place the men who are single with praying women, and many of the ministries that have been stopped are going to be rekindled and go forth. I feel strongly about this because it goes along with a vivid vision that I once saw in which there was a huge mountain. The arm of the Lord was outstretched, and His right hand was coming over the mountain. This mountain had a wooded area, but there was also a clearing where men of all ages, sizes, and types were standing, looking almost like chess pieces. I watched in this vision as God tapped one of the men and caused him to tumble over. He picked him up by the head and shoulders, and the man turned into a piece of wood.

Then I saw the Lord looking over the earth, and He placed the man beside a praying woman. I saw Him repeat this process for quite a while. If there was a woman on her knees praying, He would stand one of the men by this woman's side. The man would then turn back to human form. He would begin to pray and kneel by this woman, and the two of them would pray together.

I continued watching the vision as God did this until the mountain was nearly cleared of men. I believe this represented single men who had been praying for good, holy wives.

As I began to see other visions of men coming forth, I felt that these visions went together and signified that, in certain areas, God is going to place men in women's lives if they'll wait on God and not get ahead of Him.

Women, I know it's hard to wait sometimes, but it is a must if you want to remain in the will of God. If God has made you a promise that He has not yet fulfilled, you need to wait on it. He will fulfill His promise. He is faithful. He is just. He is a good God.

Healing

From the smallest to the largest problems, God cares about every facet of our lives, and He wants us to pray and intercede for healing. God has given us great doctors, but I also believe in healing by the Master's touch. I believe that when Jesus speaks a word of healing, whether the ailment is physical, mental, or spiritual, we are healed by His sacrifice for us.

> *He was wounded for our transgressions, He was bruised for our iniquities; the*

chastisement for our peace was upon Him,
and by His stripes we are healed.
(Isaiah 53:5)

Jesus went to the cross so that through Him and in His name, we could be healed. He is a Healer, and He is a Deliverer.

God's Love Brings Healing

Years ago, my cousins and I were guests on a television program in Tennessee, and we were talking about the reality of hell and salvation through Jesus. After the program, I went back to the house where all my other relatives were and found that they had been drinking and were stone drunk. I noticed a little dog there that was dragging its back as if it were injured or disabled, and I said, "Well, they're out of it, so let me pray for the dog." I prayed for the dog, and it started walking normally. My aunt was shocked, and she screamed, "Oh my God! I'm going to stop drinking!" That dog was healed, and it lived to a ripe old age.

From the smallest to the largest problems, God cares about our lives.

On another occasion, I was at the home of someone who owned a big boxer. This dog would come over to me and take its nose and move my hand on top of its head. At first, I thought this was very strange. Then I decided to pray for the dog. The owner of the dog came over and asked, "What are you doing?" And I said, "Well, I'm praying for your dog." She cried and said, "He has two brain tumors." When she took the dog back to the vet, the tumors were all gone. It's not as if that dog had faith. Yet it felt the anointing of God. Why? Because if something is important to us, then it's important to God. It was God's love that brought that healing. If God will heal an animal, how much more will He do for us?

Some Illness Is Demonic Affliction

One time, when I was a guest speaker overseas, the Lord opened my eyes to see the spiritual stronghold that was causing the manifestation of a child's illness. While I was preaching, I saw a dark shadow around the child's neck that resembled a serpent. I was seeing this image from a spiritual viewpoint, of course, and not from the natural. The child was about three years old, but because he had no strength in his neck, his head wobbled back and forth.

The Lord was showing me that this affliction was definitely of the devil, so I immediately began to seek the Lord and pray in the Spirit for his deliverance. As I was praying, the mother began wheeling the child in his stroller down the aisle to the front of the church. The Lord spoke to me and said, "After you preach, I want you to pray for the baby first, and you will see Me remove that serpent. The baby will be healed, but it will be a slow process because of the weakness of his little neck."

So I listened to the Lord, and after the service I went straight to the child with some assistants and prayed in English. I saw an angel come and put his hand into that dark object and jerk it off the child's neck. When he yanked it off, I could see that it looked like a black snake about two feet long. The angel held it up in his hand, and out of the air came the word of God: "By Jesus' stripes you are healed!" (See Isaiah 53:5.) The angel took the snake out of the church, and I praised God.

The child's neck was still in a weak state and his head continued to wobble, so I prayed that his neck would be strengthened and that the bones would grow straight. Whatever the Spirit told me to pray, I prayed over that child, and I anointed him with oil. I was so happy, and the mother was happy. She did not see what I saw, but I knew God had delivered him through His Word and prayer. Jesus is the Deliverer.

That little child had truly been attacked by the enemy, and this is what many people are facing today. They find themselves feeling the brunt of the enemy's brutal attacks. Often, they do not know how to counteract them. In addition, other Christians sometimes tell them that their illnesses or misfortunes are due to some sin in their lives.

It is a misconception that those who find themselves in the midst of the devil's attacks or who are facing trials have brought these things upon themselves because of wrongdoing. While it is true that we can invite self-inflicted wounds and open the door to the demonic, this is not *always* the case concerning those who fall prey to Satan's cruel blows.

Satan's darkness is no match for the light of God.

As Jesus pointed out to His disciples in John 9, the reason some people experience illnesses or other distressing situations is so that their lives may manifest God's wonderful works. When Jesus and the disciples came in contact with a blind man, the disciples asked, *"Rabbi, who sinned, this man or his parents, that he was born blind?"* (John 9:2). They automatically equated the blindness with sin. Jesus, however, was quick to set the record straight: *"Neither this man nor his parents sinned, but that the works of God should be revealed in him"* (John 9:3).

Jesus wanted the disciples to know that in spite of the man's blindness, God's light would shine through his circumstance. Satan's darkness is no match for the light of God. Jesus said, *"As long as I am in the world, I am the light of the world"* (John 9:5). He also told us we are to minister in His name and reflect that same light:

> *You are the light of the world. A city that is set on a hill cannot be hidden. Nor do they light a lamp and put it under a basket, but on a lampstand, and it gives light to all who are in the house. Let your light so shine before men, that they may see your good works and glorify your Father in heaven.* (Matthew 5:14–16)

Nothing will stop the will of God from being manifested or keep Him from being glorified. He can touch you in a way that will cause those around you to see a noticeable change as the Spirit of God shines through whatever darkness has been preventing you from seeing His truth. When Jesus healed the blind man, his neighbors recognized that a change had occurred, although it was so radical that it confused many of them. They questioned among themselves, *"'Is not this he who sat and begged?' Some said, 'This is he.' Others said, 'He is like him'"* (John 9:8–9). So the blind man—now healed—testified, *"I am he"* (John 9:9).

Just before healing the blind man, Jesus had escaped those who were about to stone Him. (See John 8:59.) Note that as one group was rejecting Jesus, one man was about to see God's light and receive a miracle. You never know when or where God is going to show up to deliver a miracle. This is why it's so important to pray and continue seeking the face of God, even when you feel like giving up.

Training in Healing

Many times, God has spoken to me about how to pray for people for healing. He began training me and foretelling things that He would show me. He would say, "Now, at times I will show you someone's body like an X-ray. And you will see a dark spot here and there, or you will see a spirit of infirmity, such as the one that was on that child's neck." And He said, "I'll teach you how to pray. You have to take dominion over the devil and bind the strong man in Jesus' name." (See Mark 3:27; Luke 11:20–22.) The Lord would go on to instruct me, "When I show you these things, I'm definitely going to heal these people who are affected by these afflictions. Remember, I don't show them to you just for you to see. I show them to you so that you may ask Me to deliver them. And I get the glory and the praise."

"Oh," I said, "Jesus, that's so easy. I want to do that, and I don't want any glory or any praise. All healing power comes from You, Lord." So that's how the Lord began to teach me about the gifts of healing and the word of knowledge. (See 1 Corinthians 12:7–9.)

Then He began to talk to me about how He would work in my services. He would put angels behind people and have me call them out and give them a word of knowledge and a prayer. He would show me signs, such as a spot on their lungs or a spot on one of their hips, and instruct me to pray, and He would heal them. He would show me an open vision of His healing power in manifestation. It was so exciting to see angels present, and God's Word coming out of the air like a sword. The Word would go into a sword and then into the dark spot of a person's body. The angels would put fire upon the spot where the illness was located and burn out that sickness. *"Who makes His angels spirits, His ministers a flame of fire"* (Psalm 104:4). It was like spiritual warfare on these bodies, delivering them from sicknesses and diseases.

Healing Signs and Wonders

God spoke to me and said, "I'm going to give you greater success in certain parts of the human body." When Jesus showed me hell, much of the time He held my left hand as we walked through the abode of the dead, and He would stop and explain things to me. Shortly after my experience in hell, this word about healing began to play out.

Five years later, God spoke to me and asked, "Do you know why I held your left hand in hell and showed you these things?" I answered, "No, Lord." He explained, "I gave you a special healing gift as a sign in the earth. When you talk about this truth of hell, I will tell you to pray for people's teeth, gums, and mouths. I will do creative miracles. I will show a sign in their mouths by miraculously repairing their gums and teeth. I will do it My way, not your way or man's way."

I was very excited and just believed that God would do what He had said. I began to pray for people's mouths and teeth in services, saying, "God is going to repair teeth." I began to get mocked and persecuted, but I didn't care. I knew that I was not a dentist and was incapable of doing these things, but I also knew that God could do anything. I began to pray for people all over the world: Australia, South America, Scotland, Canada, and so on. I began to impart my gift with some of the ministers and the leaders. Amazingly, as I prayed for people's teeth, you could actually see God filling their teeth with gold and silver.

One time, I prayed for a little baby whose front teeth were rotten. The mother couldn't afford a dentist, so I prayed for that baby's teeth, and ten minutes later God had regrown them. Witnessing this just blew our minds! I would go into Canada and minister to Native Americans. I would ask Jesus to fix their teeth, and God would miraculously replace missing teeth and fill those that were damaged with gold. This would excite us and we would shout and praise the Lord.

Continue seeking the face of God, even when you feel like giving up.

On another occasion, a young woman named Debbie had come a long way to attend one of my meetings because she had heard that God did these things. Debbie needed some teeth filled, and one of her teeth was missing. We prayed, and two weeks later she called me. She said she woke up, and God had given her a whole gold tooth in the back of her mouth. I began to shout and praise the Lord!

You never know when God is going to perform His miraculous feats. You could pray today and experience His miracle a month later. I had pastors call me from Canada, saying, "Mary, you told us what God could do, and some of us made fun of you, and we're so sorry. Three weeks after you were here, our children woke up with all their teeth repaired by the Lord, and the dentist here was amazed!" I said, "Praise the Lord! I walk by faith and not by sight."

When God chooses to begin using you as a vessel to show forth His miraculous works, He sets you aside. You begin to experience these things with the Lord, and you can't help but share them with others. These are only a few of the miraculous experiences that I have had with God through prayer.

Never Take Prayer for Granted

I want to conclude with an account that illustrates the power and mercy of the Lord on our behalf. Years ago, after my son Scott came home from the Navy, he became addicted to drugs. One day, I was away on a trip when I suddenly heard the Lord say, "I am the Way, the Resurrection, and the Life." When I heard this, I sensed in my spirit something was wrong. So I called home trying to reach my son. When I couldn't reach him, I called a prophet, a man who heard clearly God, and he told me, "Your son has died. But I see his soul coming out of his body, and God is cupping His hands around his soul and putting it back into his body. He is reconnecting the soul and the spirit. And he shall not die but live to declare the works of the Lord."

When I finally got in touch with my daughter over the phone, she was screaming, "Mom! Scott's dead. They took him to the hospital!" I responded, "Oh, no. He is not going to die. And he is going to declare the works of the Lord." Later, we got in touch with Scott. He said he had woken up in the hospital on a gurney with a sheet laid over him. So he just got up and left the hospital! It pays to pray. We should never take prayer for granted because it truly works.

Epilogue:

Changed by His Presence, Ministering through His Power

My visions of heaven revealed the magnificence of God and the abundance of His greatness. I saw rooms of teardrops, which are the tears God's people have shed, and which He has collected. (See Psalm 56:8.) I saw rewards given to us in heaven (see Revelation 22:12) and trees with leaves for the healing of the nations; as souls went into heaven, they were taken to the river of life and given the leaves of the trees to eat. (See Revelation 22:2.) I saw the throne of God high and lifted up, with a rainbow resting above it. God's garment was brilliant, and it was covered with jewels. (See Revelation 4:2–3.)

Heaven (and later the new heavens and earth) is where the redeemed reside. We will have glorified bodies, and God has prepared wonderful blessings for us. We are going to walk on streets of pure gold—what I like to call Hallelujah Boulevard. The gates to the city are made of pearls. (See Revelation 21:21.) It is a beautiful place.

> *As it is written: "No eye has seen, no ear has heard, no mind has conceived what God has prepared for those who love him"—but God has revealed it to us by his Spirit. The Spirit searches all things, even the deep things of God.*
>
> (1 Corinthians 2:9 NIV)

> *For now we see in a mirror, dimly, but then face to face. Now I know in part, but then I shall know just as I also am known.*
>
> (1 Corinthians 13:12)

This is what God has in mind for us, but we also need to love, trust, and serve Him wholeheartedly now.

> *Seek the LORD while He may be found, call upon Him while He is near. Let the wicked forsake his way, and the unrighteous man his thoughts; let him return to the LORD, and He will have mercy on him; and to our God, for He will abundantly pardon.*
>
> (Isaiah 55:6)

> [God granted] *us that we, being delivered from the hand of our enemies, might serve Him without fear, in holiness and righteousness before Him all the days of our life....*[Jesus] *will go before the face of the Lord to prepare His ways, to give knowledge of salvation to His people by the remission of their sins, through the tender mercy of our God, with which the Dayspring from on high has visited us; to give light to those who sit in darkness and the shadow of death, to guide our feet into the way of peace.*
> (Luke 1:74–79)

Whether we know it or not, we need God in every facet of our lives. He doesn't want our money or other riches; He wants us to commune with Him and participate in His divine works on earth through prayer, intercession, and other ministries. The experiences I've had in prayer have been so great that no one could ever make me discount prayer's importance.

The experiences I've had in prayer have been so great that no one could make me discount its importance.

Prayer has the ability to transform us and society. As we commune with the Lord, we are changed by the power of His presence. We discover who we are and what God's purposes are for us, so we may fulfill His will for us on earth. This is the day of spiritual manifestation when prayers are going to be answered more rapidly than ever before. Therefore, we must prepare ourselves not only to receive from God, but also to share the importance of prayer with others.

This almighty God whom we serve must be lifted up.

> *Glory in His holy name; let the hearts of those rejoice who seek the Lord! Seek the Lord and His strength; seek His face evermore!* (1 Chronicles 16:10–11)

Throughout our many travels, we have had the opportunity to witness the power of prayer upon those to whom we have ministered. Our prayer is that you will embrace the valuable truths and principles of this book and use them in your daily life. May you not only find the material that you have read informative, but may it penetrate your spirit so you may begin to experience the blessings and power of God through prayer.

Jesus said,

> *Assuredly, I say to you, if you have faith as a mustard seed, you will say to this mountain, "Move from here to there," and it will move; and nothing will be impossible for you.* (Matthew 17:20)

In verse 21, Jesus reminded the disciples that the demon they had been trying to cast out could be removed only by prayer and fasting. (See verse 21.) First, however, He wanted them to understand the power of faith. It takes faith only the size of a mustard seed to move insurmountable obstacles. When we remember that it is God who is moving the mountains and not ourselves, this statement suddenly begins to make sense. Prayer is empowering because it is not the words we say that cast out demons, cause healing, or bring salvation. Rather, it is our connection to God, through Christ, who responds to our love for Him, our faith in Him, and our obedience in doing His will.

> *Prayers are answered through our connection to God, who responds to our love, faith, and obedience in doing His will.*

Please pray with us.

Prayer of Agreement

Heavenly Father,

We pray in the name of Jesus that the prayers of this reader will be answered according to Your divine will. May Your peace, which passes all understanding, and Your anointing overtake him or her right now. Allow the words that he or she has read to become a permanent presence, and endow your servant with power from on high to overcome every obstacle that attempts to hinder success in his or her life. May this reader reach a new level of anointing that equips him or her to pull down strongholds and have victory in every facet of life.

In Jesus' name, amen.

—*Mary K. Baxter* and *George G. Bloomer*

Appendix:

YOUR STRATEGIC PLAN FOR PRAYER

It is necessary to have a strategic plan to incorporate prayer into your life. Learning to pray and practicing prayer do not come automatically. Yet, as we have seen, prayer is essential for our spiritual lives. As we begin to view prayer as a way of life rather than as a religious ritual, as we develop an increasingly close relationship with the Father, and as we experience the power of prayer, we will no longer try to force it into our hectic schedules but instead will begin to build our lives around it.

The following are some guidelines for developing a life of prayer based on the truths and principles in *A Divine Revelation of Prayer*, including reflection questions and strategic plan ideas corresponding to each chapter. We suggest that you purchase a spiral or loose-leaf notebook or journal in which you can write your responses to the reflection questions, as well plan your personal strategy for incorporating prayer into your life. Then, use what you have written to review your progress and growth, and to record answers to prayer, as you move forward in your relationship with your heavenly Father.

Chapter 1: Is God Really Listening?

Reflecting on Prayer:

- What is your everyday experience of prayer like?
- In the past, if your prayers haven't seemed to have been answered, how has this affected your relationship with God?
- In what ways have you given up on God? Have you stopped believing that God will answer a certain prayer? Why?
- What are some reasons the answers to your prayers may not yet have manifested?
- What God accomplishes in the spiritual realm will be manifested in the physical realm in His timing as we pray and have faith in Him. How does this knowledge change the way you think about "unanswered" prayer?

Your Strategic Plan:

1. Put God first by spending quality time with Him. Just pour out your heart to Him, be honest with Him, and give Him your life. If you've been angry with Him because you thought He wasn't answering your prayers, ask Him to forgive you and to fill you with His love.
2. What changes do you need in your life? Write down some of the things that you have been too

afraid to talk to God about and begin to pray over them daily for complete deliverance. Then watch as God begins to miraculously move mountains in your life and give you His power.

3. When it seems as if God isn't listening, faith must lead the way until the manifestation of what you have been praying for becomes a visible reality. The role of faith is to transfer us from a human way of thinking to a spiritual mind-set, so that we no longer think or act based upon our physical limitations. What does God's Word say about your most pressing situation? What does it say God will do for you as you trust in Him?
4. Focus on God, not the circumstances.

> *Now to Him who is able to do exceedingly abundantly above all that we ask or think, according to the power that works in us, to Him be glory in the church by Christ Jesus to all generations, forever and ever. Amen.* (Ephesians 3:20–21)

5. The most important component of prayer is having a relationship with God through Jesus Christ. If you don't have this relationship and want a new start to your life, you can have that right now by praying this prayer with a sincere heart:

Lord Jesus, I need a new start today. I know You have been dealing with me, and I need You more today than ever before. In Your name, I humbly come to You. I believe that You are the Son of God and that You died for my sins. Forgive me of all my sins. I surrender my heart to You, Lord Jesus. Come into my heart, and fill me with Your Holy Spirit. Lead me and guide me. Thank You for the new start that You have given to me on this day. Amen.

You can write a personal prayer here:

Thought:

Turning back to God is only a prayer away.

Chapter 2: The "How" Is Up to God

Reflecting on Prayer:

- What answers to prayer have you recognized only sometime after you received them?
- When have the answers to your prayers come in a form you did not expect?
- Do you usually want God to answer your prayers in a specific way? If so, in what way?
- How do you react toward God when He answers in a way you don't expect—or don't like?
- Do you really believe God has your best interests at heart? Why or why not?

Your Strategic Plan:

1. The Word of God is just as alive today as it has ever been, but our reluctance to believe it often gets in the way of our receiving what God wants for us. Offer God your requests, based on His Word, and then step back and allow Him to answer your prayers according to His divine will and in His own way. Don't ask how He will answer, but instead thank Him for answering.
2. You will not receive the benefits of prayer by constantly giving up on God. Read and meditate on Scriptures affirming that God is the ultimate Promise Keeper. (See, for example, Psalm 119:160; 2 Peter 1:3–4; Hebrews 10:23.)

3. With gratitude, thank God for answers to prayer that you did not expect or appreciate at the time but now realize were in your best interests.
4. Don't give up! (See, for example, Luke 18:1 and Galatians 6:9.)

Thought:

God always has a greater picture in mind than we can see.

Chapter 3: Seeking Answers in False Gods

Reflecting on Prayer:

- Have you looked to human or demonic sources for answers for your life? Which ones? What was the reason you gave up on God?
- If you have considered astrology and the paranormal as either harmless fun or compatible with Christianity, what is your opinion of them now that you have read chapter three?
- What are the consequences of involvement in demonic activities and rituals?
- Have you ever wanted a sign from God more than a true relationship with Him, as the Pharisees did? If so, why?

- Why might God not give you information about the future?

Your Strategic Plan:

1. Sincerely repent and ask God to forgive you if you have engaged in any form of psychic activity, demonic ritual, divination, witchcraft, or other aspect of the occult or paranormal.
2. Instead of seeking answers in false and demonic sources, ask God to give you His wisdom and understanding for your life. Acknowledge to God that He is your true Source. (See Isaiah 45:6.) Let His voice be the one you listen to.
3. Consider how you have been trying to control your life rather than letting God lead and guide you. Then release control of your life to God and trust Him with your present and your future. Meditate on such Scriptures as Deuteronomy 33:26–27 and Romans 8:35–39.
4. Instead of worrying about how things in your life will turn out, concentrate on loving, trusting, and serving God, being assured of His complete love for you. (See Jeremiah 29:11; Acts 1:7–8; Ephesians 3:17–19; 1 John 4:16; Isaiah 26:3–4.)
5. Read and study the Word of God so you will not be deceived by those who claim they know and love God but are engaged in ungodly practices.

Thought:

For God has not given us a spirit of fear, but of power and of love and of a sound mind.

(2 Timothy 1:7)

Chapter 4: Communing with the Father

Reflecting on Prayer:

- Does God have first priority in your life? Have your recognized your need for regular time alone with Him to worship and hear from Him?
- What distracts you from communing with Your heavenly Father?
- What does it mean to "pray without ceasing"?
- What are the benefits of communing with the heavenly Father?
- What are some of the keys to determining God's true voice in prayer?
- How will our communion with God help other people, as well?

Your Strategic Plan:

1. List the distractions that hinder you from communing with God. Then make provision for dealing with these distractions, whether it means talking with God silently when others are around, making a special room for prayer,

putting a "Do Not Disturb" sign on your door, turning off the television, unplugging the telephone, clearing your mind of the busyness of the day, or other provisions.

2. Seek oneness with God by praying that His thoughts will become your thoughts, and that His ways will become your ways. (See Psalm 1:1–3; Isaiah 55:8–9.) Then continue to read, study, meditate on, and obey His Word so that you continually take in His knowledge and wisdom.

3. Pray for yourself and others what Paul prayed for the Ephesians, so that you and they may be spiritually strengthened by communing with the Father through the Holy Spirit:

   > *I pray that out of his glorious riches he may strengthen you with power through his Spirit in your inner being, so that Christ may dwell in your hearts through faith.* (Ephesians 3:16–17 NIV)

4. As you pray, make sure that you not only give God your requests, but that you also listen to Him by giving Him time to speak to you as you wait in quietness. Remember to evaluate thoughts and impressions you receive according to the guidelines on pages 94–95.

5. Set aside times of prayer to worship your heavenly Father and praise Him for His goodness.

6. Develop a lifestyle of open communion with God throughout the day by making yourself continually available to Him for prayer and service, and by constantly keeping in touch with His presence, acknowledging Him in all things.

Thought:

"For who is he who will devote himself to be close to me?" declares the Lord.

(Jeremiah 30:21 NIV)

Chapter 5: Lord, Help Me to Pray!

Reflecting on Prayer:

- What are the disadvantages of lacking true humility?
- Have you ever announced to others or affirmed to yourself what God was going to do in your life and then immediately been attacked by the enemy with doubt or discouragement? How did you respond?
- Have you ever prayed to show off or seem "spiritual" in the eyes of others? How do you feel when you see other people do this? What do we miss out on when we pray in this way?

- How would you pray differently if you kept in mind that God knows your needs before you ask? (See Matthew 6:7–8.)
- Do you agree with this statement: "Whatever God's will is for my life, it is right"? Why or why not?
- If you have a tendency to rejoice only when things are going well, in what ways can you learn to rejoice during difficult times?

Your Strategic Plan:

1. When the enemy attacks you with doubt or discouragement regarding God's will and promises for you, ask God to give you His strength and guidance to stay on track and not give up believing.
2. To keep open communication with God, repent and ask forgiveness for all known sins in your life and recommit to pursuing the character and ways of God. Also ask God to reveal your hidden sins so you may repent of them. (See Psalm 19:12–13 NIV.)
3. Review Jesus' pattern for prayer in Matthew 6:9–13, as well as the material related to it in chapter five. Even though the words may be familiar, read them again and consider them carefully. Then incorporate their themes and truths into your daily prayers.

4. Jesus gave us a beautiful example of submission to the Father when He prayed, *"Not My will, but Yours, be done"* (Luke 22:42). Do you have a hard time releasing control of your life to God? Are you wasting time with things that are not His will? Remember that the tower of Babel was a waste of time and money and resulted in confusion and disarray in the lives of the participants. (See Genesis 11.) Ask God to give you a desire to pursue His will. David prayed, *"Restore to me the joy of your salvation and grant me a willing spirit, to sustain me"* (Psalm 51:12 NIV). We have this assurance in Philippians 2:13: *"For it is God who works in you both to will and to do for His good pleasure."*
5. Make a list of things in your life you are thankful for. Then offer your gratitude to God.
6. Jesus' model prayer ends with, *"For Yours is the kingdom and the power and the glory forever. Amen"* (Matthew 6:13). Incorporate heartfelt worship, praise, and thanksgiving into your daily prayers.

THOUGHT:

"Your kingdom come. Your will be done on earth as it is in heaven."

(Matthew 6:10)

Chapter 6: Overcoming Hindrances to Answered Prayer

Reflecting on Prayer:

- What do prideful people try to avoid? What do they inevitably draw to themselves? (See Proverbs 11:2.)
- Mary Baxter said that forgiveness was a prerequisite for her to receive revelations from God. Why do you think that was so?
- Why is it that, often, we are confronted by more challenges the more we grow in the Word of God?
- What should you do when you make mistakes or fall in relation to your Christian walk? How can mistakes be used for good in our lives?
- Mary Baxter talked about the "lure demon" that seduces people into behavior that is destructive and against God's will and purposes. In what area of your life do you have the most difficulty resisting temptation?
- What is the best defense against hindrances to answered prayer?

Your Strategic Plan:

1. Each of us struggles with certain areas more than others. Yet all of us battle in some way with every one of the following hindrances to answered prayer. Review each of these areas,

asking God to reveal how they may be affecting your relationship with Him and other people, as well as your personal well-being. Ask Him to enable you to overcome them through His Spirit and to fill you with the fruit of the Spirit instead. (See Romans 8:13–14; Galatians 5:22–23.)

- *Lack of a Pure Heart* (including dishonesty with God, covering up your true nature, and denying your real condition)
- *Ignoring "Weightier Matters"* (including complacency toward sin; focusing on religious ritual and superficialities rather than on love, compassion, and justice according to God's nature)
- *Anger and Unforgiveness* (including bitterness, a lack of love toward others, holding on to grudges, and being easily offended)
- *Pride* (including not admitting your mistakes, not taking initiative to correct your mistakes or change your behavior, and hardening your heart toward God)
- *Lack of Spiritual Growth* (including spiritual apathy, not having been born again and received God's Spirit to enable you to grow, not progressing from the *"milk"* of the Word to the *"meat"* of the Word. [See 1 Corinthians 3:2; Hebrews 5:12–14.])

2. In whatever area you have the most difficulty resisting temptation, pray for the grace and

blood of Jesus to cover you, for deliverance in the name of Jesus from any demonic force of control behind it, and for the ability to resist the temptation through the power of the Spirit.

THOUGHT:

If by the Spirit you put to death the deeds of the body, you will live. For as many as are led by the Spirit of God, these are sons of God.

(Romans 8:13–14)

CHAPTER 7: A SACRIFICED LIFE

Reflecting on Prayer:

- How often do you spend time alone with God in intimacy and quietness? What has been your experience when you have done this?
- Do you purposely go to God with your problems and concerns, or do you usually rely only on family, friends, acquaintances, or people in the media for advice about your life?
- Are you experiencing any spiritual pain from pulling away from God and not obeying His Word when you could be drawing closer to Him?
- What did Mary Baxter learn about the "sacrificed life" and "dying to ourselves" from the vision she received?

- What is the surest place to find rest in the midst of stress and trials?

Your Strategic Plan:

1. Taking the "yoke" of Jesus enables us to have peace and strength in the midst of life's trials and problems. It also helps us to develop much-needed intimacy with Him. Accept Jesus' invitation from Matthew 11:28–30 and receive refreshment and rest from His presence and guidance in your life.

   - *"Come to Me"*: Yield your will to Jesus and acknowledge Him as Lord of your life. Spend time in the Father's presence, coming to Him in the name of Jesus. Unburden yourself, giving your problems to Him and asking Him for advice and direction for your life.
   - *"Take My yoke upon You"*: Ask the Father, in the name of Jesus, to help you to recognize any burden in your life that is not from Him. Pray that He will help you to release it and change your perspective and priorities to match His will for you. We cannot do everything in life, so ask Him to help you see what you are meant to do, and then to do it in His strength.
   - *"Learn of Me"*: Take time regularly to sit quietly in Jesus' presence through prayer and to learn how to become familiar with His voice

and receive His wisdom, knowledge, and guidance. Commit to spending time reading the Word so you can learn God's true thoughts and ways. Ask the Holy Spirit to bring to your remembrance what you have read in the Word that you particularly need for your current life situations.

2. The sacrifice involved in fulfilling God's calling upon your life includes making time to pray, study His Word, and intercede for yourself and others. Ask God to help you do this as you follow the leading of His Spirit. Sacrifice is not something rigid. God wants you to have balance and abundant life. (See John 10:10.) Sacrifice will involve dying to our selfish desires and sinful natures and replacing them with God's desires and ways. Yet it is ultimately freeing and joyful. Ask God to enable you to offer your life as a complete and acceptable sacrifice to Him, and to remain yielded to Him.

THOUGHT:

I beseech you therefore, brethren, by the mercies of God, that you present your bodies a living sacrifice, holy, acceptable to God, which is your reasonable service.

(Romans 12:1)

Chapter 8: Attitudes and Qualities of Intercessors

Reflecting on Prayer:

- Are you willing to "stand in the gap" and pray for our country and our world at a time when many people lack reverence for God and are turning from Him to engage in destructive lifestyles? (See Ezekiel 22:29–30.)
- How does the knowledge that Jesus and the Holy Spirit are interceding for you change your perspective and your practice of prayer in relation to yourself and others?
- What do you think of J. Rodman Williams's statement "Compassion is the wellspring of miracles"? Who in your life needs you to show them the compassion of God?
- Have you ever "wrestled" in prayer for someone? (See Colossians 4:12 NIV.)
- According to this chapter, what is the one component that sets apart those who have great power in prayer from those who continually seek others to pray for them?

Your Strategic Plan:

1. When you intercede for yourself and others, incorporate the themes Jesus used when He prayed for all believers in John 17. Jesus prayed (1) that believers would live in unity, just as He

is one with the Father, (2) that we would have the same joy He has, (3) that we would be kept from the evil one, (4) that we would be sanctified by God's truth, (5) that we would have unity with other believers and with the Father and the Son, (6) that we would be witnesses to the world of the truth of the gospel because of this unity, and (7) that one day we would live with Jesus and see His glory.

2. Ask the Father to baptize you in the Holy Spirit to help you to pray according to His will, either in your native language or in a Spirit-given prayer language.
3. Review chapter eight, focusing on each of the qualities of effective intercessors and seeking to develop it in your own life:
   - *Alignment with Jesus and the Holy Spirit:* Are you praying for God's kingdom to come and His will to be done on earth as it is in heaven? (See Matthew 6:10.)
   - *Willingness and Faithfulness:* Do you have a willingness to intercede on behalf of God's work in the world and are you faithful in doing so? (See, for example, Colossians 4:2 NIV.)
   - *Reverence for God and Righteousness:* Do you honor God's name, and are you in right relationship with Him? (See, for example, 1 Corinthians 6:16–7:1.)

- *Knowledge of Who God Is:* Do you know the power and greatness of God? (See, for example, 2 Kings 19:15.)
- *Knowledge of Who You Are in God:* Do you know who you are as a child of God through Christ Jesus? (See, for example, Colossians 2:10; Romans 8:16–17.)
- *Faith:* Are you allowing your reading of God's Word to build your faith? (See Romans 10:17.) Are you relying not on your earthly sight but upon the vision of God? (See Hebrews 11:1.)
- *Compassion:* Are you following Jesus' example of responding to people's needs with empathy and praying for others with God's compassion? (See, for example, Matthew 9:36–38.)
- *Persistence and Perseverance:* Do you give up and turn from God when you encounter struggles or when you stumble and fall? Or do you press on, reaching out to God and asking Him to restore you and to make you an overcomer? (See, for example, Luke 18:1–8; Galatians 6:9.)

4. Make a point to persevere in prayer for other people and their needs, as Paul said Epaphras did for the Colossians: *"He is always wrestling in prayer for you, that you may stand firm in all the will of God, mature and fully assured"* (Colossians 4:12 NIV).

THOUGHT:

Prayer has the power to set the captives free because it connects the intercessor to the All-powerful One.

CHAPTER 9: VISIONS OF DELIVERANCE AND ANSWERED PRAYERS

Reflecting on Prayer:

- When your loved ones or others are going through difficult times that they have brought on themselves or when they are behaving in self-destructive ways, how should you pray for them? How should you not pray for them?
- Why do demons sometimes engage angels in conflict after we have prayed? How should we respond to such attacks?
- How do we know that the devil has already been defeated in his plans to overthrow the kingdom of God? (See, for example, Revelation 12:7–11; 20:2–3, 10; Luke 10:17–20; Colossians 2:15.)
- What did Mary Baxter say Jesus showed her was the reason many people are in hell today? How should we respond to this?
- For what needs should we intercede, as highlighted in this chapter?

Your Strategic Plan:

1. Are you putting off salvation, thinking that you will be saved "tomorrow"? Answer the question Elijah put to the Israelites, and receive Jesus as your Lord and Savior today. (See 1 Kings 18:21.) Do not let Satan deceive you into believing you can live your life without a true relationship with God and then come to Him whenever you feel like it. Don't wait until it's too late. Be reconciled to God and become a new creation in Christ. (See 2 Corinthians 5:17.)

2. Intercede for others you know who are being hindered from fulfilling the call of God on their lives, as the men in Mary's visions were. Ask God to free them from their hindrances and to bring them out of their captivity. Pray that they would obey God, that their relationships would be restored, that their families would be blessed, and that the Lord would bring healing to every issue in their lives. Pray that they would get involved in good churches that teach the Word of God and that they would maintain focus on God and do His will.

3. Ask God to give you discernment in praying for people's healing and deliverance, so that you can pray specifically according to the need (for example, physical cause, special situation

through which God will be glorified, demonic attack).

4. Pray for the "smaller" needs you see around you and build your faith for the greater problems. God cares about all our concerns, whether small or large. You will grow in your knowledge and experience of prayer, so start putting prayer into practice and see what God will do!

THOUGHT:

Satan's darkness is no match for the light of God.

About the Authors

Mary K. Baxter

Mary Katherine Baxter was born in Chattanooga, Tennessee. While she was still young, her mother taught her about Jesus Christ and His salvation. At the age of nineteen, she was born again.

In 1976, while she was living in Belleville, Michigan, Jesus appeared to her in human form, as well as in visions and revelations. During those visits, He revealed to her the depths, degrees, levels, and torments of lost souls in hell, telling her that this message is for the whole world. Since that time, she has received many visitations from the Lord. In God's wisdom, to give balance to her message, she has also received many visions, dreams, and revelations of heaven, angels, and the end of time.

On Mary's tours of hell, she walked with Jesus and talked with many people. Jesus showed her what happens to unrepentant souls when they die and what happens to servants of God when they do not remain obedient to their calling, go back into a life of sin, and refuse to repent.

Mary was ordained as a minister in 1983 at a Full Gospel church in Taylor, Michigan. Ministers, leaders, and saints of the Lord around the world speak very highly of her and her ministry. The movement of the Holy Spirit is emphasized in all her services, and many miracles have occurred in them. The gifts of the Holy Spirit with demonstrations of power are manifested in her meetings as the Spirit of God leads and empowers her.

Mary loves the Lord with everything she has—all her heart, mind, soul, and strength. She is truly a dedicated handmaiden of the Lord, and she desires above all to be a soulwinner for Jesus Christ. From the headquarters of Divine Revelation, Inc., her Florida-based ministry, this anointed evangelist continues to travel the world, telling her story of heaven and hell and her revelatory visits from the Lord.

For speaking engagements, please contact:
Evangelist Mary K. Baxter
Divine Revelation, Inc.
P.O. Box 121524
West Melbourne, FL 32912-1524
mkbaxter@adivinerevelation.org
www.adivinerevelation.org

About the Authors

Bishop George G. Bloomer

Bishop George G. Bloomer is the founder and senior pastor of Bethel Family Worship Center, a multicultural congregation in Durham, North Carolina, and The Life Church in Goldsboro, North Carolina. He can be seen weekly on his national television broadcast, *Spiritual Authority.*

A native of Brooklyn, New York, Bloomer overcame difficult personal challenges, as well as a destructive environment of poverty and drugs, and he uses those learning experiences as priceless tools for empowering others to excel beyond their seeming limitations. He travels extensively as a conference speaker, and he conducts many seminars dealing with relationships, finances, stress management, and spiritual warfare.

Bloomer is the author of a number of books, including *Looking for Love, More of Him, Authority Abusers,* and the national best seller, *Witchcraft in the Pews.* He has previously collaborated with Mary K. Baxter on *A Divine Revelation of Deliverance,* their first book together.

He has appeared as a guest on several television, radio, and media outlets nationwide, including CNN's *Faces of Faith*, The Trinity Broadcasting Network, *The Harvest Show* (LeSEA Broadcasting), and *The 700 Club* (Christian Broadcasting Network).

Bishop Bloomer has been awarded an honorary Doctor of Divinity degree from Christian Outreach Bible Institute. He resides in Durham with his wife and two daughters.

Mary Baxter shows how many lives have been forever transformed by the power of Jesus' blood. Whatever your situation, you can have new intimacy with your heavenly Father and receive miraculous answers to your prayers—through *The Power of the Blood.*

The Power of the Blood
Mary K. Baxter with Dr. T. L. Lowery
ISBN: 978-0-88368-989-9 • Trade • 272 pages

A Divine Revelation of the Spirit Realm
Mary K. Baxter with Dr. T. L. Lowery
ISBN: 978-0-88368-623-2 • Trade • 208 pages

Mary Baxter gives a unique perspective into the angelic and demonic realms. In vivid detail, she describes her encounters with spiritual beings, both good and bad, as she shares anointed insights into conducting spiritual warfare. This is the strategy manual for spiritual warfare!

www.whitakerhouse.com